Skills for Better Reading
< Advanced >

構造で読む英文エッセイ〔上級編〕

Yumiko Ishitani

NAN'UN-DO

Skills for Better Reading
<Advanced>

Download Audio
音声ファイル
無料 DL
のご案内

このテキストの音声を無料で視聴（ストリーミング）・ダウンロードできます。自習用音声としてご活用ください。
以下のサイトにアクセスしてテキスト番号で検索してください。

https://nanun-do.com　テキスト番号［**511642**］

※ 無線 LAN（WiFi）に接続してのご利用を推奨いたします。

※ 音声ダウンロードは Zip ファイルでの提供になります。
お使いの機器によっては別途ソフトウェア（アプリケーション）の導入が必要となります。

Skills for Better Reading <Advanced> 音声ダウンロードページは
左記の QR コードからもご利用になれます。

1 構造で読む英文エッセイ

本書の目的は、「全体的なエッセイ構造を考えながら内容を掴む」ということを体得することにあります。そうすることによって、少し内容の難しい英文でも速く読むことができるはずです。英文においては、それぞれのエッセイにはそれぞれ目的があり、論理によって進んでいく、ということが、日本文よりも明確です。それぞれのパラグラフに役割があり、その組み合わせで、ひとつの目的に向かって進んでいるということを掴んでください。本書はそれぞれのパラグラフがどのような役割をもっているのかに重点を置いて作られています。4つの典型的なエッセイ構造を提示しておりますが、この基本を身につけることによって、次にどのような内容のパラグラフがくるのか、筆者がどういう方向に行こうとしているのかを推測する力がついてくるはずです。

もちろん、新聞・雑誌の英文では、こうした基本的パターンをさまざまに崩したものも使われております。本書では、4段落でひとつのまとまりが基本ですが、実際にはその他にさまざまな役割をもった段落が差し挟まれているのが通常です。または基本4段落の中のひと段落がいくつかの段落に分けられていることが実際にはほとんどです。そのことをふまえた上で、それでも根底を流れている基本パターンを掴むことが内容理解には非常に大切なことです。

また、この基本エッセイパターンを理解することは、エッセイ・ライティングにも非常に役立ちます。今回、本書ではそれぞれの課の一番最後に、テーマとなっているエッセイパターンを使って、自分でエッセイの骨組みを作ってみるブレイン・ストーミングが配置されています。これを基にしてエッセイを書いてみるというさらに上の段階へ進んでほしいと思います。

これまで ***Skills for Better Reading*** のシリーズとしては、標準、社会科学（Social Sciences)、自然科学（Science and Technology）が刊行されています。本書はこのシリーズの一環として、さらに上の「上級（Advanced)」となります。それぞれのニーズに合わせて使っていただけたら幸いです。

2 ここで扱う 4 つのエッセイパターン

このテキストでは、エッセイのパターンを次の 4 つの型に分けています。

1　意見サポート型
2　パラグラフ並列型
3　直線型
4　異質パラグラフ型

次に、それぞれのパラグラフがそれぞれのエッセイの中でどのような役割を果たすかということについて、簡単に図示してみましょう。

第 1 のパターン：意見サポート型

Unit 1 ~ 3

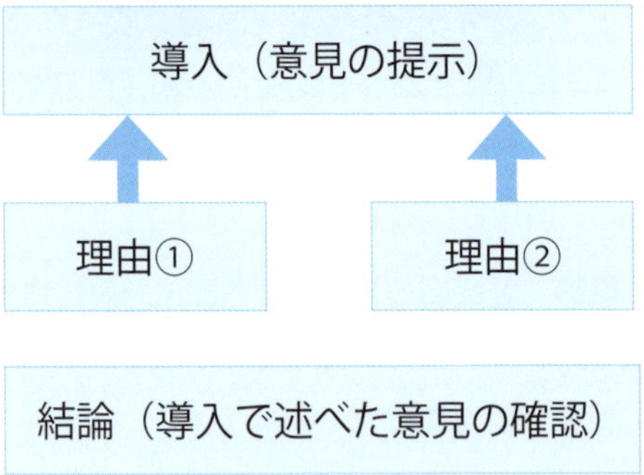

最初に自分の意見を明確にし、それを支える理由をその後の段落で述べていくパターン。最後の段落では最初に述べた意見をもう一度確認します。このテキストでは、1 ～ 3 課で次の 3 種類を提示します。

1 結論・理由
2 社会事象の説明
3 結果・原因

第 2 のパターン：パラグラフ並列型

Unit 4 ~ 7

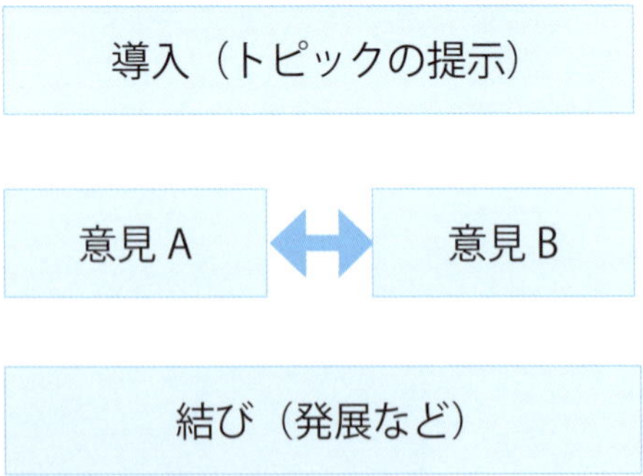

トピックを説明するいくつかのパラグラフがそれぞれ同じ重要性をもって並列に配置されるエッセイパターンです。それぞれのパラグラフは相対関係にあります。このテキストでは、4 ～ 7 課で次の 4 種類を提示します。

4 複数の意見
5 比較
6 賛成・反対
7 分類

第3のパターン：直線型

Unit 8～10

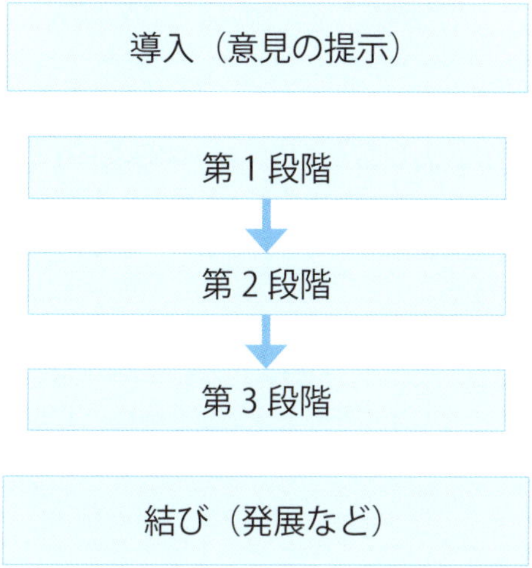

時間の流れに沿って順に説明をしていくものです。このテキストでは、8～10課で次の3種類を提示します。

8 歴史
9 過程
10 原因ー結果

第4のパターン：異質パラグラフ型

Unit 11～14

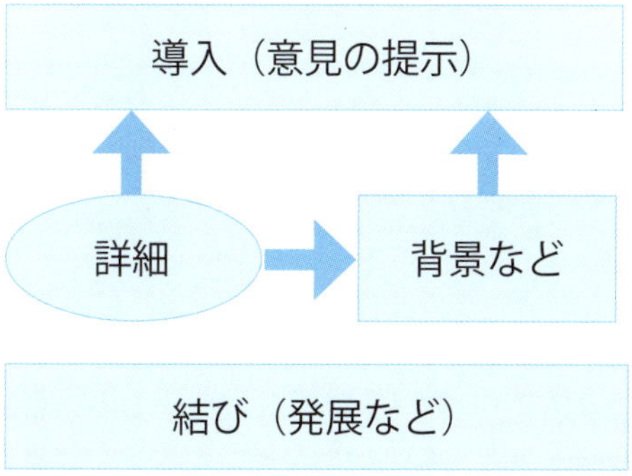

役割の違う複数のパラグラフで構成するエッセイパターンです。このテキストでは11～14課で次の4種類を提示します。

11 問題解決
12 言葉の定義
13 実験
14 新製品

3 本書の使い方

本書はそれぞれの課が6ページ構成になっています。

第1ページ

エッセイのおおまかな構造を掴んでください。ひとつのエッセイがどういう流れで構成されているのかに着目してください。

第2ページ

そこで取り扱われる構成パターンを使った読みもの Reading A があります。テーマとなっている構造を頭に入れながら読んでください。Reading Aの目的は、エッセイ構造に着目するためのものです。

第3ページ

Reading Aのエッセイ構造図を完成させてください。これでエッセイの全体像が見えるはずです。また、英文の要約をつけてあるので、キーワードを埋めていくことで大まかな内容を英語で理解できます。

第4ページ

もうひとつの読み物、Reading B です。こちらも、その課でテーマになっているエッセイ構造となっていますが、Reading A よりも長く難しい内容です。構造を頭に入れながら、細かい内容にも注意を向けて読んでください。

第5ページ

Reading B に対応した問題をつけてあります。第1問で、それぞれのパラグラフの内容を日本語で確認する問題を付しておりますので、ここでだいたいのエッセイ構造が掴めるはずです。

第6ページ

Reading B の内容確認問題です。すべて英語の質問であり、英語で答えるようになっています。

各パートの扉ページとまとめ問題ページ

本書ではエッセイの構造を大きく4つにまとめて表示しています。それぞれのパートの一番最初のページに、そのパートに共通するエッセイ構造図が示されています。それぞれのパートの一番最後のページにはそのパートのエッセイ構造を使って自分でエッセイ構造を書いてみることができるようにいくつかの問題をつけておきました。エッセイ構造を簡単に作ってみたらそれを利用して英文エッセイにチャレンジしてみることもできます。

本書はあくまでも、全体的な内容を掴むということを目的にしております。細かいところを気にせずに、パラグラフのポイント、ポイントを素早く掴むということが重要です。もちろんさらに Reading 力をつけるためには、精読も必要ですので、あとで英文の細かな分析を行うこともお勧めします。

Contents

Part I

1 Conclusion / Reasons 11
理由で押し切る！

A. Fuel-Only Corn
B. Is the Right Brain More Important than the Left?

2 Social Phenomenon 17
社会現象を説明する

A. "No Toilet, No Bride" Campaign in India
B. Macedonian Naming Dispute

3 Result / Cause 23
原因を究明する

A. Dreams Come True
B. Boys' Toys and Girls' Toys

Part II

4 Several Explanations 31
いくつかの説明

A. Northern People Have Bigger Brains
B. Gold Fish Magic

5 Comparison 37
比べてみよう！

A. Macau and Hong Kong
B. Comparison of Right of Succession in the U.K. and Japan

6 For and Against 43
賛成と反対

A. Should the Smallpox Virus be Kept?
B. Was Dropping the Atomic Bombs Right?

7 Classification 49
分類してみよう！

A. Tea
B. Folk Tales

Part III

8 History 57
歴史をたどる

A. History of Coffee
B. History of the Weekend

9 Process 63
過程を説明

A. How to Play Kabaddi
B. How to Select an American President

10 Cause and Effect 69
原因と結果

A. Uganda: a Banana Republic
B. Detroit Bankruptcy

Part IV

11 Problem Solving 77
問題解決

A. "Paradox"
B. Monty Hall Problem

12 Definition of a New Word 83
最近気になる言葉を考えよう

A. "Galapagos Syndrome"
B. Rare Earth

13 Experiment 89
実験で証明

A. Rats also Have Sympathy
B. Indian DNA

14 New Product 95
新製品

A. Blue Rose
B. Coca-Cola

Part I

エッセイ構成：意見サポート型

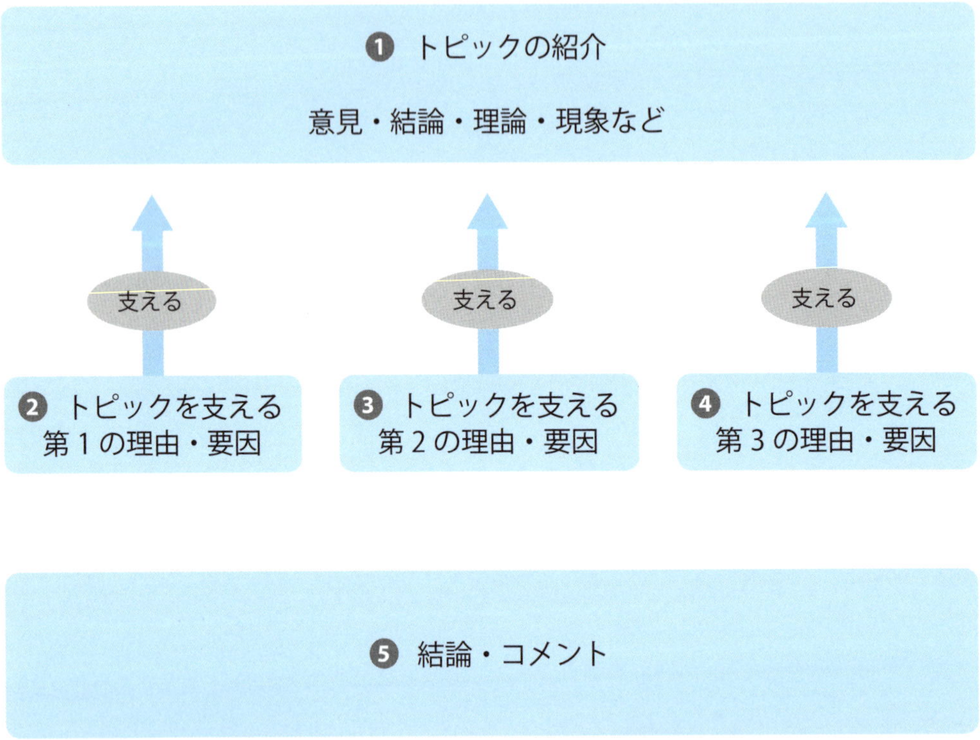

最初のエッセイパターンは、筆者の意見、社会現象、自然現象などをとりあげ、それを正当化または確認するために、それを支える理由、原因、要因などをいくつか提案して、読み手を納得させることを目的としたものです。TOEFL や IELTS、または欧米の大学で課されるエッセイのパターンとしては一番使われるものです。「結論はこれだ。なぜならばこれこれこういう理由だからだ」は最も一般的な欧米の思考形式で、結論をあいまいにしがちな日本的様式と対照的なところです。

Conclusion / Reasons

理由で押し切る！

1

エッセイ構成：意見サポート型

❶ トピックの紹介

意見・結論

↑ 支える ↑ 支える ↑ 支える

❷ 意見を支える
第１の理由

❸ 意見を支える
第２の理由

❹ 意見を支える
第３の理由

❺ 結論

①で述べた意見・結論を確認

論議を呼んでいる問題について、自分はそれについて「賛成だ」または「反対だ」として自分の意見を明確にして、それを正当化するために、いくつかの理由を出し、最後に「こういうわけで自分はこの結論に達した」と締めるエッセイです。欧米の大学のレポートを書く上で基本的なパターンですし、最も典型的な欧米式思考様式です。エッセイに限らず、スピーチやディベートなどでも活用できる様式です。

A. Fuel-Only Corn

02

[1] One of the biggest problems the U.S. faces today is securing a steady supply of energy. The U.S. now depends on other countries for half of its energy requirements. Nuclear power might be the first choice to consider as a solution, but nuclear energy is fraught with controversy. So what other options are there? Some researchers have been turning their attention to "fuel-only corn oil." It is now possible to produce a genetically modified (GM) corn that can be used to produce fuel for various energy needs. Promoters maintain that this type of corn is a perfect energy resource that burns without smoke, odor, or ash, and, as a result, causes no air pollution. In my opinion, however, fuel-only GM corn is not the solution and should not be promoted.

[2] I have several reasons for believing this, but they can be narrowed down to two. The first is that fuel-only corn can potentially worsen the global food crisis. Because of recent unstable weather, harvests have declined worldwide, and a great number of people around the globe are suffering from hunger and famine. The U.S. is one of the world's primary food-exporting countries, and many developing countries have long relied on America's vast, rich croplands for food. The trend that sees American farmers transferring their cropland into land for growing GM corn for fuel only is a disaster for the huge number of starving people in developing countries. It is estimated that most of the corn grown in the U.S. is so-called commercial corn, which is used for soft drinks, cattle feed, and fuel for automobiles. Some researchers say that only about one percent of U.S.-produced corn is used for food to be consumed directly by humans. If this trend continues, less and less food will be produced, which will lead to rapidly rising food prices. As a result, more people will suffer from starvation, creating a critical international humanitarian issue.

[3] The second reason why I believe GM corn should not be produced for fuel only is that the growing process may cause cross-contamination in the environment. GM corn contains an added gene for an enzyme called amylase that speeds the breakdown of starches into ethanol. Many ecologically concerned people contend that GM corn may affect existing food-for-consumption corn crops by cross-pollinating with them. If pollen from GM corn moves into fields where natural corn plants are growing, and cross-pollination occurs, the natural corn will gain an extra gene, which will then spread to other corn plants. This could pose a serious danger to anyone who eats the corn.

[4] Environmental pollution is a serious problem, one that we need to tackle by seeking and developing clean energy sources. Fuel-only corn offers one possibility, but if it endangers humans and puts lives at risk by reducing worldwide food supplies, we should by all means reconsider it.

❶ 左の文章の内容をまとめてみよう。

① 導入（結論）

② 理由 1

③ 理由 2

④ 結論

❷ Fill in the blanks to summarize each paragraph.

1 The U.S. needs an alternative energy source, but (n   ) energy may not be the solution because of the dangers it poses. (G   ) modified corn could be one possibility because it can be used to produce fuel that won't (p   ) the air. However, I am against the use of this method for two main reasons.

2 The first is that fuel-only corn will (r   ) the amount of food available for human consumption all over the world, which could cause widespread famine.

3 My second reason is that GM corn may affect natural food-corn crops by cross-(p   ) with them. Eating such contaminated corn can be harmful to human health.

4 Thus, because fuel-only corn could potentially put humans in danger, I believe that it should (n   ) be promoted.

Notes

1 secure 確実にする　steady 安定した　be fraught with ... …を伴う　controversy 論議　fuel-only corn oil 燃料コーン油　genetically modified 遺伝子組み替えの　promoter 推進者　odor におい

2 be narrowed down to ... …に集約される　potentially もしかすると　worsen 悪化させる　famine 飢饉　cropland 耕地　transfer A into B AをBに変える　disaster 災難　critical 深刻な　humanitarian 人道的な

3 cross-contamination 相互汚染　enzyme 酵素　amylase アミラーゼ　breakdown 分解　starch 澱粉　ethanol エタノール　contend 主張する　cross-pollination 異花受粉　pose 引き起こす

4 tackle 取り組む　endanger 危険にさらす　put ~ at risk ～を危険にさらす　by all means 絶対に

B. Is the Right Brain More Important than the Left?

03

1 Are you a "right-brain" person or a "left-brain" person? Science has already confirmed and explained that the right side of the brain and the left side of the brain control different fields of mental activity. In general, the left brain is linked to linear reasoning and language function. In contrast, the right brain is involved in the processing of visual and audio stimuli, dealing with spatial concepts and facial perception, and controlling artistic ability. Based on the results of recent neuroscientific research, many people now assume that a left-brain person is more logical and even more intelligent than a right-brain person. In a technological society like ours, where logical and intelligent people have a greater chance of achieving success, people tend to think more highly of left-brainers. But there are some researchers who believe that the right brain is more important than the left brain when it comes to increasing a person's chances of survival in today's society.

2 The first reason is that the right brain is capable of seeing the big picture, of taking in what is happening as a whole, while the left brain focuses on narrower, more particular issues. The right brain channels and processes all incoming data, deciding which is important and which is not. Thus, the right brain is deeply connected with and involved in the real world. Interestingly, the right brain usually knows what the left is doing, like a mother watching over her child. The left brain, however, usually has no idea what its right counterpart is doing, or what is going on in the outside world.

3 The second reason some cite for the right brain's superiority is that the right brain processes negative feelings and emotions. According to some scientists, when we are depressed, the right brain works to remove or reduce our negative feelings and emotions. The left brain, meanwhile, only processes pleasurable experiences. Of course, we need positive emotions—otherwise, we would never feel happy. But if depression isn't dealt with and properly treated, it can lead to death. If our negative emotions take over and get out of control, we may contemplate suicide. So being able to deal with and process negative emotions becomes, literally, a matter of life and death and makes the right brain an essential survival tool.

4 The third factor that comes into play is that the right brain is an all-rounder. This means that the right brain can make up the left brain's function. You can live without the left brain, but not without the right brain. Patients with right-brain strokes are not capable of recognizing what has happened to their bodies. Patients with left-brain strokes, however, can see what their bodies are undergoing. This is because the right brain does the left brain's job when the left brain is damaged.

5 The fourth reason is that the right brain makes human relations better. Language is said to be the left brain's responsibility, but the right brain has quite adequate understanding of what people say, even when the left brain misses it. In

fact, the left brain misses many aspects of linguistic meaning. For example, the left brain cannot "get" jokes or pick up on unspoken implications. But the right brain doesn't miss a thing.

[6] The two main categorical functions of the right brain and the left brain—comprehensiveness and precision, respectively—are of course both necessary for human beings to live. But as we've seen, perhaps the right brain is more important for survival. The left brain is a specialist; the right brain is an all-rounder. This comprehensiveness is why some people think the right brain is more important than the left.

❶ それぞれの段落について、次の質問に答えなさい。

[1] 左脳と右脳の機能をそれぞれ簡潔に述べなさい。

左脳：＿＿＿＿＿＿＿＿

右脳：＿＿＿＿＿＿＿＿

[2] 生存のためには右脳人間の方がいいという第 1 の理由は？

＿＿＿＿＿＿＿＿

[3] 第 2 の理由は？

＿＿＿＿＿＿＿＿

[4] 第 3 の理由は？

＿＿＿＿＿＿＿＿

[5] 第 4 の理由は？

＿＿＿＿＿＿＿＿

[6] 右脳と左脳の機能をそれぞれ簡潔に言うと何と何か？

＿＿＿＿＿＿＿＿

Notes

[1] confirm 確認する　linear reasoning 直線論法　stimuli (stimulus の複数形) 刺激　spatial 空間的 perception 認知　neuroscientific 神経科学の　assume 思う　think highly of ... …を高く評価する
[2] take in 理解する　channel 導く　counterpart 相手方
[3] superiority 優位性　remove 排除する　meanwhile 他方　pleasurable 楽しい　take over 指導権をとる contemplate 考える　suicide 自殺　literally 文字通り
[4] come into play 働く　all-rounder 万能者　stroke 脳出血　undergo 行う
[5] adequate 十分な　aspect 様相　pick up on 気づく　implication 意味　not a thing 全然～ない
[6] comprehensiveness 総合理解　precision 正確さ　respectively 各々

2 Write "R" next to the factors or traits that refer to the right brain. Write "L" next to those that describe the left brain.

1. reasoning ( ) 2. language ( )
3. spatial conception ( ) 4. facial perception ( )
5. intelligence ( ) 6. artists ( )
7. a higher chance of success in technological society ( )
8. control of negative feelings ( )
9. an all-rounder ( )
10. "getting" jokes and implications ( )
11. comprehensiveness ( ) 12. precision ( )
13. a specialist ( )

3 True or False

1. The left brain is related to language ability, but without the right brain, it would be difficult for us to understand unspoken implications. T F
2. The left brain decides which incoming data is important and which is not. T F
3. When you are happy, it is the right brain that processes your feeling. T F
4. Patients with right-brain strokes can't understand what is happening around them. T F
5. The writer thinks that the left brain is more directly related to the matter of suicide or survival than the right brain, which is why the left brain is more important. T F

LEFT & RIGHT BRAIN

Social Phenomenon
社会現象を説明する

2

エッセイ構成：意見サポート型

❶ トピックの紹介
ある社会現象の提示

↑ 支える ↑ 支える ↑ 支える

❷ 原因 1
その現象を引き起こした
第 1 の原因

❸ 原因 2
その現象を引き起こした
第 2 の原因

❹ 原因 3
その現象を引き起こした
第 3 の原因

❺ まとめ

トピックとなる社会現象を紹介し、その現象が現れた社会的原因・背景をいくつか提示していくパターンです。それぞれあげる原因が、トピックとなる社会現象を説明し、支える構成となっています。社会科学系学部で課されるエッセイにとても有効なエッセイ構成です。社会現象にはさまざまな要素が原因として考えられます。それらの要素をうまく３つくらいにまとめてトピックとなる社会現象の出現を説明してみましょう。

A. "No Toilet, No Bride" Campaign in India

04

1 Can you imagine living in a house without a toilet? If you were a new bride, would you want to go and live in such a house? Well, if you were in India, you might very well have to. While the Indian government is aiding households to ensure that each has a toilet, progress is still slow. For newly married women, not having a toilet in the house is one of the worst possible conditions. But because an Indian woman's status has traditionally been very low in her husband's home, the woman of the house has not been able to demand a toilet. But the situation is gradually getting better. Recently, a campaign with the slogan, "If you don't have a toilet at home, you can't get a bride," has been helping to improve sanitary conditions and women's status. What has inspired the Indian women's rights movements? Several factors are involved.

2 The first is education. Nowadays, more and more Indian women go to school thanks to the general modernization of society, steady economic development, and the government's efforts to make education available to everyone. India is one of the world's fastest-developing countries, especially in the field of information technology. The government is therefore eager to educate the country's population, enabling more people to contribute to economic development. This trend has allowed more women to get jobs and to gain the economic power they need to support themselves. This financial independence has made it possible for many women to marry at a later age or even to remain unmarried. For a long time, Indian women had little choice but to marry a man who would give them a place to live. The misery Indian women have endured has been the focus of much attention. Traditionally, fathers have had to pay a cash gift known as a "dowry" to their daughters' future husbands. It goes without saying that this has been a heavy financial burden on the fathers. But now, because of the increase in women's economic power, many Indian women are able to choose whether to marry or not.

3 The second reason for the rise of women's rights in India is that the country has many more boys than girls. In traditional Indian society, boys have been preferred to girls. A girl will eventually leave home and need a "dowry" when she marries. A girl is, in other words, a burden for her family economically, which is why so many girl babies have been killed at birth. But now, because boys far outnumber girls, a woman has a large selection of possible grooms to choose from. Thus, a man who wants to marry is forced to accept his bride's demand for a toilet at home.

4 The third reason is the spread of television and the Internet. A huge flood of information and ideas from around the globe has shown Indian women how women in other places live and has allowed them to make comparisons with their own situation. They can see modern houses and lifestyles and learn about Western ideas such as human and women's rights, gender equality, and so on. They now realize that for most people outside their own society, living in a house without a toilet is unthinkable—impossible!

5 For these reasons, women in India are coming up in the world. Their new-found economic independence, improved education, and knowledge of the world at large make it only natural that they demand a toilet when they get married. Surely, it's not too much to ask.

1 左の文章の内容をまとめてみよう。

① どんな社会現象？ → ② 原因 1 → ③ 原因 2 → ④ 原因 3 → ⑤ まとめ

2 Fill in the blanks to summarize each paragraph.

1 The lack of toilets in homes has been a serious problem in India, but now women have started to demand that there be a toilet in their husband's house after (m   ).

2 The first reason for this new movement is that more and more women are being educated, enabling them to claim their (r   ).

3 The second reason is that India's long history of preference for boy children means that the number of boys (o   ) that of girls, which also means that brides are more in demand.

4 The third reason is that Indian girls have become more enlightened thanks to a flood of outside information over the (I   ) and on TV.

5 As a result of Indian women gaining more economic independence and higher (e   ), they have started to claim their rights.

Notes

1 might very well ... …する可能性が高い　aid ~ to V ～がVすることを助ける　ensure ～を確かなものにさせる sanitary 衛生の

2 available to ... …の手に入る　have little choice but to V Vする以外にほとんど選択肢がない　misery 悲惨さ　endure 耐える　It goes without saying that S + V ... …は言うまでもない　burden 負担

3 eventually いつかは　outnumber 数のうえで上回る

5 come up in the world 出世する　at large 一般的に

B. Macedonian Naming Dispute

05

[1] Have you heard of the country called Macedonia? You no doubt studied world history in school, so you must be familiar with Alexander the Great, the Greek king who built the Macedonian Empire in the 4th century B.C. Today, the Republic of Macedonia still exists as an independent nation, and is perhaps best known as the birthplace of Mother Theresa. But in ancient times, the area that is now the Republic of Macedonia existed on the northern edge of the Macedonian Empire, which meant that it was just a border area and not the main part of the Macedonian Empire. Today, the fact that the people living in this area call their country "Macedonia" has caused a dispute with people living in Greece, who claim they have the right to use the name "Macedonia" as a part of their culture.

[2] In 1913, after the Balkan wars, the area where ancient Macedonia was located was divided into three parts: Greek Macedonia, Bulgarian Macedonia, and Serbian Macedonia. Serbian Macedonia became part of Yugoslavia after World War II, but after the breakup of Yugoslavia in 1991, Serbian Macedonia became an independent country and was re-named the "Republic of Macedonia." Greece, however, did not approve of or accept this name. Macedonia became a member state of the United Nations in 1993, but in the U.N. it is called the "Former Yugoslav Republic of Macedonia" because of the dispute with Greece over its name. This growing tension between the Republic of Macedonia and Greece is now an issue with international significance and possible serious repercussions. Why does Greece so fiercely refuse to accept this name?

[3] The first reason is that Greeks believe that historically speaking, Macedonia is inseparably associated with Greek culture. They therefore contend that only Greeks have the right to use the name today, since the southern Slavs that now live in the area arrived 1,000 years after the Macedonian Empire collapsed. Therefore, these Slavs, say the Greeks, don't have any connection with ancient Macedonia and are not in any way the descendants of ancient Macedonians. The Greek view stresses that the name Macedonia is most suitable for the southern part of ancient Macedonia, which is now the northern province of present-day Greece (including the capital of the ancient kingdom, Pella), and also known as Macedonia. Ancient Macedonia, Greeks say, started in this area, but not the Republic of Macedonia, which was later added to the Macedonian Empire and, later still, was invaded by Slavs and other peoples. In a nutshell, the Greeks think that the homeland of the Macedonian Empire is now a part of Greece. Alexander the Great and the ancient Macedonians were Greek, and, today's Greeks contend, only the northern Greek province of Macedonia should be the "real Macedonia."

[4] Another reason for the Greeks' opposition to the name is that they fear that the Republic of Macedonia will try to expand its territory to Greek Macedonia

and Bulgarian Macedonia under the name of "Greater Macedonia." In fact, Greece believes that the Republic of Macedonia chose the name precisely because it has territorial ambitions. This has been a serious Greek concern for decades. In April 2008, the foreign minister of Greece raised objections when the prime minister of the Republic of Macedonia appeared in a photograph next to a map of "Greater Macedonia."

5 Now the Republic of Macedonia has launched a campaign called "Antiquisation" as a way to put pressure on Greece and, at the same time, to build a sense of national identity and pride among its people. Statues of Alexander the Great and his father Philip, who conquered much of Greece, have been put up in several cities. Many public buildings such as airports, highways, and stadiums have been renamed after Alexander and Philip. These actions are clearly intended to aggravate Greece. For outsiders, the Greece-Macedonia quarrel may just seem like a simple local naming dispute. But for the countries involved, this issue runs deep.

1 それぞれの段落について、次の質問に答えなさい。

1 昔のマケドニア帝国と現在のマケドニア共和国は地理的にどのような違いがあるか？

____

2 Serbian Macedonia が「マケドニア共和国」と名乗れない理由とは？

____

3 ギリシア人が、旧ユーゴスラビア領マケドニア共和国が「マケドニア」と自称するのがいやな第 1 の理由は？

____

4 第 2 の理由は？

____

5 マケドニアは「古代化」を計っているが、その例をあげなさい。

____

Notes

1 edge 端　dispute 論争
2 breakup 崩壊　approve of ... …を承認する　repercussion 影響　firecely 熱烈に
3 inseparably 密接に　contend 主張する　collapse 倒れる　not in any way 絶対に～でない　descendant 子孫　invade 侵入する　in a nutshell 要するに
4 territory 領土　concern 懸念　objection 反対
5 launch 始める　antiquisation 古代化　conquer 征服する　put up 建てる　statue 彫像　aggravate 怒らせる

❷ Complete the following chart describing the history of the "Republic of Macedonia (RM)."

① The 1( ) part of the Macedonian Empire. →	② Serbian Macedonia was born in 2( ). →	③ Serbian Macedonia became one part of 3( ) after WWII. ↓
⑥ RM is now officially called the "Former Yugoslav Republic of Macedonia" because of its naming dispute with 6( ).	← ⑤ RM joined the U.N. in 5( ).	← ④ The Republic of Macedonia was born in 4( ).

❸ Fill in the blanks.

Greeks today don't like Serbian Macedonians calling their country the "Republic of Macedonia" because Greeks believe the name "Macedonia" is deeply connected to their own culture and history, and that only 1(G) have the right to use that name. Historically, the people who live in the Republic of Macedonia are not actually Greeks, but 2(S), and the Greek people think its residents are not actual 3(d) of ancient Macedonia. To Greeks, only the Greek province of Macedonia can be legitimately called "Macedonia." Greek people also fear that the government of the Republic of Macedonia aims to expand the republic's territory and will try to claim the 4(n) part of Greece as its own. The fact that the Republic of Macedonia is now putting up many statues of Alexander the Great and his 5(f) Philip in the republic has made Greeks even more skeptical about the ambitions of the Republic of Macedonia.

Result / Cause

原因を究明する

3

エッセイ構成

❶ トピックの紹介

❷ 結果
ある事象・事件・問題

↑ 支える

❸ 原因
それを引き起こした原因

❹ まとめ

身近に起こるある事象や社会問題を取り上げ、それが起きた原因を究明するエッセイです。Lesson 2 の Social Phenomenon「社会事象を説明する」では、考えられるいくつかの理由で、ひとつの社会現象を支えていましたが、この Lesson では、ひとつの決定的な原因で「結果」を説明します。「結果」から「原因」と進めるエッセイ構造ですが、もちろん「原因」→「結果」へと進める方法もあります。このパラグラフ順にすると Part 3 の時系列順となり、Lesson 10 の Cause & Effect「原因から結果へ」のパラグラフ構成となります。

A. Dreams Come True

06

1 Did you have a dream while you were sleeping last night? If so, can you tell us what the dream was about? If you can, the dream must have had a strong impact on you, because, as everybody knows, most of the time, as soon as we get up in the morning and start to go about our daily business, we forget the dream.

2 There are many questions about dreams that have yet to be answered. One of the most intriguing has to do with the fact that we have all had the experience where a dream we had actually comes true! For example, one night you meet an old friend in a dream, and the next day you actually run into that friend on the street! How can this phenomenon be true? Is it just a coincidence? Perhaps not. Recent neuroscientific research shows that there is a scientific explanation.

3 Sleep scientists have discovered that we have an average of about four dreams each night. They take place every 90 minutes or so, and each one lasts around 20 minutes. But when we wake up, we forget most of these nocturnal "stories." We think that we have forgotten all our dreams, but they are actually stored somewhere in our brain. Let's say that one day we hear about a car accident, and we remember a dream we once had that matches the news. From this, we somehow come to think that our dream predicted the car accident, causing us to believe that we have the power of prophecy. We have forgotten that we have had many other dreams in between as well. Then, to make matters worse, we subconsciously twist the content of the dream to match what has really happened. Dreams are by nature vague, because we have them while we are sleeping. This means there is a lot of room for us to add in other information, as well as to twist the content of our dreams to match what happened afterwards, which makes our dreams seem closer to the actual event. All of which makes us believe that our dreams have come true, while, in reality, it is just a matter of probability.

4 Sleep scientists have discovered that around 80 percent of dreams are far from "sweet." That's why we are far more likely to relate bad news in dreams to what actually happens in real life, and why so many dreams seem to predict death or disaster. But why do we have more bad dreams than good dreams? If we had more good dreams, life would be more pleasant, wouldn't it? Our knowledge of dreams and sleep is still quite limited, and there are still many more mysteries to be solved. But as science reveals more and more secrets of our brain, we will learn many more truths about these experiences.

1 左の文章の内容をまとめてみよう。

① 導入	→	② 結果
		↓
④ 結び	←	③ その理由・原因

2 Fill in the blanks to summarize each paragraph.

1 We have many dreams, but we almost immediately (f　　　　　　　　) most of them.

2 Some dreams we have seem to actually (h　　　　　　　　) in real life.

3 We have many dreams every night, and they are all stored somewhere in our (b　　　　　　　　). When something happens in real life, we subconsciously connect it with the dream we have had.

4 Since we have more (b　　　　　　　　) dreams than good, it's only natural that so many of our dreams predict or have to do with death or disaster.

Notes

1 go about ... …に取りかかる
2 intriguing おもしろい　run into ... …に出くわす　coincidence 偶然の一致
3 nocturnal 夜の　somehow どういうわけか　prophecy 予言　to make matters worse さらに悪いことに subconsciously 潜在意識的に　twist ねじまげる　by nature もともと　vague 漠然とした　add in ... …を加える
4 relate ~ to ... ～を…に結びつける　reveal 暴露する

B. Boys' Toys and Girls' Toys

07

1 Boys are active, girls are quiet; boys like colors such as black, blue, and gray, while girls like red, pink, and yellow; boys love baseball and soccer; girls love reading and writing. Are these images and conclusions all just stereotypes? Some people say they are the result of social norms, which means that social pressure makes boys and girls make such "predictable" choices. In other words, girls and boys take it for granted that they should behave the way society and their peers expect them to. For example, if a boy wears a pink shirt to kindergarten, other children will probably laugh at him, saying that he is wearing a girl's shirt, so the boy will stick to black or blue.

2 Boys' and girls' preferences for certain toys develop in the same way. They choose, either consciously or unconsciously, toy cars and dolls, respectively, because of social pressure. "I am a girl, so I should play with dolls like the other girls who are playing with dolls," a girl thinks. "I am a boy, so I will be laughed at if I play with dolls," says a boy. "Mother, Father, Grandmother, and others all give me dolls, so I have to play with them," a girl thinks. "Other boys are playing with toy cars in the park, so I should join them," a boy reasons. It cannot be denied that many boys and girls behave and think in this way because society and their peers pressure them into it. Some researchers, however, have come up with a scientific explanation for this phenomenon.

3 A recent study reached an interesting conclusion: this tendency for girl-boy differentiation is not only evident in human beings. In certain experiments, male monkeys also prefer to play with toy cars while the female monkeys prefer dolls. This research with monkeys strongly suggests a biological explanation for children's toy preferences. New research on human babies seems to substantiate this biological origin. Studies show that babies' exposure to hormones while they are still in the womb causes their toy preferences to emerge soon after birth. In 2009, Gerianne Alexander, a professor of psychology at Texas A&M University, tested a three-year old boy's testosterone levels. He found that they correlated with the boy's level of interest in certain toys. The higher his testosterone levels were, the more time he spent looking at "boy" toys such as trucks and various sports balls, and the less time he spent looking at dolls. According to Professor Alexander, such "boy" toys have primitive roots or meanings. They are suitable for hunting, for showing where and how far away the hunted game is, and so on.

4 What toys did you play with when you were a child? Isn't it interesting to think that your preference in toys is deeply rooted in your genes? *Why Men Don't Listen and Women Can't Read Maps*, by Allan Pease and Barbara Pease (2001), is a best-selling and widely read book that aims to show that the differences in abilities between men and women are the result of their ancient roles: hunting and rearing children. Men are good at reading maps because they have better spatial navigation abilities, which

developed with their role as hunters. Women listen to and get along with other people better because that ability was beneficial for raising children. This research might explain the reason why boys prefer cars and balls while girls prefer dolls.

❶ それぞれの段落について、次の質問に答えなさい。

1 なぜ、色や活動の嗜好に男女差があるのか？

____

2 男女でおもちゃの嗜好が違うことについての社会的な説明とは？

____

3 おもちゃの嗜好と男性ホルモンの関係を説明しなさい。

____

4 Allan and Barbara の理論を説明しなさい。

____

Notes

1 norm 規範　predictable 予想可能な　peer 仲間　stick to ... …に執着する
2 preference 嗜好　respectively それぞれ　reason 考える　come up with ... …を考えつく
3 tendency 傾向　differentiation 区別　evident 明らかな　substantiate 実証する　exposure 露出　womb 子宮　emerge 出現する　testosterone テスタステロン（男性ホルモン）　correlate with ~ ～と相互関係がある
4 navigation 航行　beneficial 利益のある

❷ Fill in the blanks.

1. A recent study shows that different toy preferences between boys and girls can also be seen in (m   ).
2. Another research study shows that how much babies are exposed to certain (h   ) while in the womb determines their toy preference.
3. Gerianne Alexander says that a boy's testosterone level is what determines his level of (i   ) in boys' toys.
4. Gerianne Alexander says that boys' toys are suitable for (h   ).
5. Allan Pease and Barbara Pease say that men are better at (h   ) and women are better at (r   ) children.

❸ If the statement is related to boys, write *B*. If it is related to girls, write *G*.

1. black, blue, and gray	( )	2. reading and writing	( )
3. testosterone	( )	4. sports balls	( )
5. spatial navigation abilities	( )	6. communication	( )
7. listening to other people	( )	8. social skills	( )
9. hunting	( )		

TRY

Write your own Essay!!

つぎのタイトルでエッセイの構成を考えてみよう。

この課で扱ったエッセイ構造を使って、自分でエッセイ構造を考えてみよう。次のエッセイタイトルを使って簡単にエッセイ構造を考え、ポイントを日本語で書いてみよう。余裕があればそれを英文のエッセイにしてみよう。

1 Conclusion / Reasons

1. 日本で遺伝子組み換え食品の推進に賛成か反対か。
   Should GM foods be allowed in Japan?
2. クローン技術の開発は社会にとって有益か否か。
   Is cloning good or bad for society?
3. 夫婦別姓に賛成か反対か。
   Should wives be allowed to keep their maiden names?
4. 消費税の値上げに賛成か反対か。
   Should the consumption tax be raised?

2 Social Phenomenon

1. 結婚しない女性が増えている。それはなぜか？
   More and more women today are choosing not to marry. Why?
2. 就職せずにアルバイトで生活する若者が増えている。それはなぜか？
   Many young people today are choosing part-time over full-time work. Why?
3. 留学する若者が減ってきた。それはなぜか？
   Fewer young Japanese are going abroad to study. Why?

3 Result / Cause

1. キリンの首はなぜ長いのか？
   Why does a giraffe have a long neck?
2. なぜ英語が世界言語になったのか？
   Why has English become a global language?
3. 日本はどのようにして経済的に成功したのか？
   How did Japan become an economic power?

Part II

エッセイ構成：パラグラフ対照型

❶ トピックの紹介

対照　　対照

❷ 第１の意見・グループ ⇔ ❸ 第２の意見・グループ ⇔ ❹ 第３の意見・グループ

❺ まとめ・コメント

Part II のエッセイパターンは、ボディとなる各パラグラフがそれぞれ比較・対照の関係になっているものです。トピックに関して、いくつかの説明を比較対照してみる、似たものを比べてみる、またあるトピックに対して、賛成意見と反対意見を書き手の判断を示すことなく平等に述べてみる、何かをある基準に基づいて分類してみる、などがこれにあたります。

Several Explanations

いくつかの説明

4

エッセイ構成：パラグラフ対照型

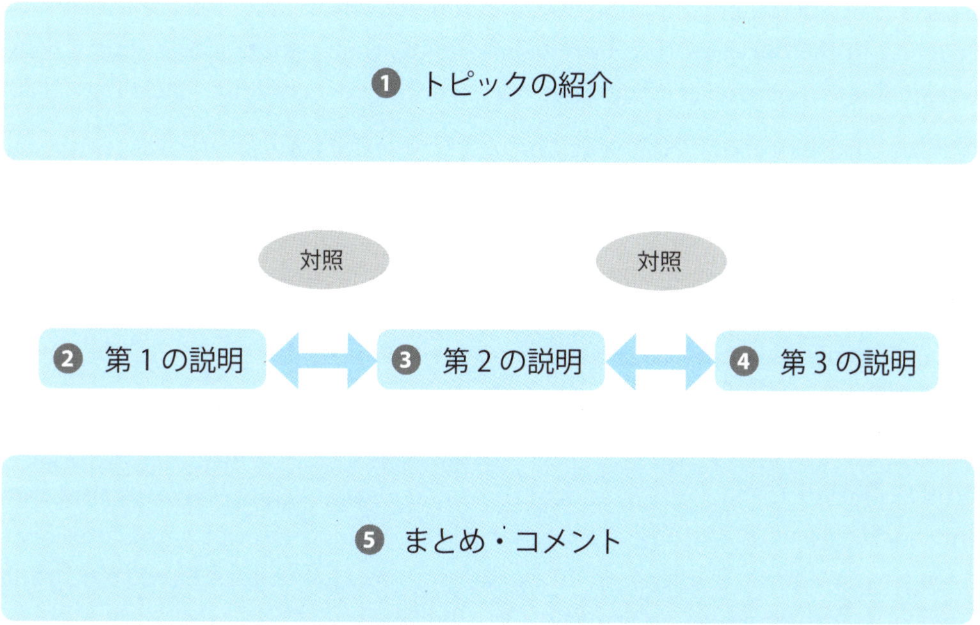

なにかの現象を提示し、なぜその現象が起きたのか、いくつかの可能性のある説明を紹介するエッセイパターンです。本書の第２課（社会現象を説明する）、第３課（自然現象を説明する）と違うところは、それぞれの説明が相反することです。Part I ではいくつかの要因がその現象を引き起こしている、ということであり、Part II で扱う「いくつかの説明」は、それぞれの原因が、独立して、相反しているということです。

A. Northern People Have Bigger Brains

08

1 Some researchers at Oxford University recently made a surprising find by examining 55 skulls preserved at the Oxford University Museum of Natural History. The skull samples were from Australia, England, China, Kenya, Micronesia, and Scandinavia and were thought to date back to the 19th century. The purpose of the study was to explore the relationship between the size of a skull and the nationality of its "owner." Does skull size change according to nationality? The results of the study suggest that, Yes, it does. The biggest brains, averaging 1,484 milliliters, were from Scandinavia, while the smallest brains, around 1,200 milliliters, came from Micronesia, which points to the conclusion that people living in the north tend to have bigger brains than people in the south. How can this be explained? Some researchers have been working to answer this puzzling question.

2 Pearce and Dumbar (2011) at Oxford University suggest that as you move away from the equator, there's less light available, so humans have had to evolve bigger eyes. This would imply that their brains also need to be bigger to deal with and process the extra visual input. Thus, say Pearce and Dumbar, there is a close relationship between less light and a bigger brain. This seems logical, but the two Oxford researchers also say that having bigger brains doesn't necessarily mean that high-latitude humans are smarter. Dimmer light requires larger eyes, which in turn requires larger visual cortices in the brain. That's all that can be said on this point.

3 But Hoffecker (2002) offers another possible explanation. He says that hunting distance increases with latitude: the higher the latitude, the fewer game animals there are to hunt per square kilometer. In such open areas, hunters have to store larger amounts of spatiotemporal information in their brains. They must remember where landmarks are, recall previous hunting routes and itineraries, and carry out mental calculation of possible movements by game animals over space and time. In places where game is hard to find, hunters' brains need to develop to allow them to collect and process increased amounts of useful information. This, says Hoffecker, is why higher latitude people have larger brains. According to another study, human brains have actually grown smaller since people started adopting agricultural lifestyles, which seems to suggest that agricultural people don't need to deal with as much visual information as hunting people do, and consequently don't require such large brains.

4 The third explanation is even more interesting. Owing to climate and geographical factors, women living at higher latitudes gather less food; in the Arctic, they gather almost none. They can't expect to find so much food in or on the ground when the men are away hunting. So what do women do at home? They engage in special tasks such as garment making, food processing, and shelter building. This sort of "family workshop" creates chances for greater technological complexity, which in turn increases natural selection for greater cognitive performance.

5 Despite these three intriguing hypotheses, researchers have still not found

a definitive answer to the question of why higher-latitude brains are bigger. It is interesting to note that this phenomenon is true of birds as well as humans. Birds at higher latitudes have bigger eyes than those living in the lower latitudes. Can we explain this by saying that it is because there is less sunlight? Do they need their larger eyes to help them find food in the dimmer light? Or is it because they have developed certain "technological" skills at home in their nests?

1 左の文章の内容をまとめてみよう。

① 導入（結論） → ② Pearce and Dumber 説 → ③ Hofecker 説 → ④ 第 3 の説 → ⑤ 結び

2 Fill in the blanks to summarize each paragraph.

1 A research study conducted at Oxford University showed that people living in the (n　　　　　　　　) tend to have bigger brains than those in the (s　　　　　　　　).

2 Pearce and Dumbar say that because there is (l　　　　　　　　) light in the north, people there have evolved bigger eyes to give them more visual input.

3 Hoffecker's hypothesis is that because (h　　　　　　　　) is harder in the north than in the south, northern people have developed bigger brains to help them collect and process useful information.

4 The third explanation is that because they can't find enough (f　　　　　　　　) outside, women in the far north have had to develop certain craft skills in the home, which has given them bigger brains.

5 No definitive answer to this question has been found, although the fact that (b　　　　　　　　) in the north also have bigger eyes may give us a hint.

Notes

1 skull 頭蓋骨　date back to 起源は～にさかのぼる　explore 探索する　puzzling 困惑させるような

2 equator 赤道　evolve 進化させる　not necessarily 必ずしも～というわけではない　latitude 緯度　dim うす暗い　in turn 一方で　cortices（cortex の複数形）皮質

3 game animal 狩り用の動物　spatiotemporal 時空的な　landmark 目印　itinerary 旅程　process 処理する　adopt 採用する　consequently その結果

4 engage in ... …に従事する　garment 衣服　shelter 住処　complexity 複雑さ　cognitive 認知の

5 intriguing おもしろい　hypotheses（hypothesis の複数形）仮説

B. Gold Fish Magic

09

[1] A magic show that was shown on "China Central Television's New Year Special" amazed the audience, who sat in awe as goldfish performed a military dance. At the same time, the show gave rise to a heated animal-rights dispute over the way the owner treats the fish.

[2] The show was performed by a magician named Fu Yongdong. For this particular trick, Mr. Fu takes six goldfish and releases them into a shallow tank filled with water, where they are free to swim around. But to everyone's surprise, the fish swim in perfect unison, lining up in a military formation and swimming laps in the tank. TV viewers were amazed at this magic trick and wanted to know how it was done. But Mr. Fu has kept this secret and so far has not revealed how the trick was accomplished. Naturally, this has prompted many people to try to figure out how the trick works.

[3] Some people say that Mr. Fu uses magnets to make his goldfish perform so unnaturally—so "unfish-like." He must somehow put magnets in the fish's stomachs, they say. How does he do this? Perhaps, they speculate, he coats iron fillings with food and forces the goldfish to eat it. Then there is either a machine or a person under the table on which the tank rests. The machine or man is holding magnets and uses them to move the goldfish with the iron fillings in their stomachs. But Magician Fu insists that his goldfish have never eaten iron fillings. If they had, he points out, the fish would look distressed. They would be in pain, or not be able to swim at all. But the fish look healthy and well.

[4] Some people argue that the trick is possible because the goldfish are not real fish. They are fake. They must be mechanical fish moved by a battery or something similar. This sounds feasible, but the show was performed in front of millions of viewers on TV. Is it possible to trick them all? Other magicians who were watching the show agree that this cannot be how the trick is done.

[5] The third hypothesis involves using a mirror in the water. Yes, if Mr. Fu used a mirror, this strange military-like performance by the fish might be explained .... But wait! This could only be true if there were only two fish. But as we have seen, there were several fish involved, all dancing and marching in synchronization. How can so many fish move in such perfect synch?

[6] Some people contend that the magician makes shadows with his hands over the fish, and the fish respond to changes in the overhead light. If the fish move as the magician wants, he feeds them as a reward. But are fish really clever enough to respond to shadows? Some people say that it is impossible to train goldfish in the same way that we train dogs. Then perhaps Fu trained the fish to follow a "leader fish" and to imitate him exactly. But it is ridiculous to expect such a high level of intelligence from a mere fish. It's unrealistic.

[7] Mr. Fu has not revealed his secret yet, and why should he? Magicians do not like to reveal their tricks .... While this magic show has prompted a lot of discussion about how the trick works, it has also raised an unexpected issue. Mr. Fu has stirred up a campaign by Chinese animal rights groups. They sent a letter to the TV channel that broadcast the show, demanding to know how the trick worked, and asking the magician to stop his "cruel" show. They believed that Mr. Fu was abusing his goldfish by, for example, forcing them to swallow magnets or training them too hard. Mr. Fu denied the accusation that he was doing something wrong, telling one news program: "If I used magnets, the fish would stick together." True. He also said, "Some people say I use electricity or high technology. They can say what they want, but the fish are safe." Magic tricks should be kept secret, but how long will Mr. Fu be able to keep the secret of his dancing fish safe?

❶ それぞれの段落について、次の質問に答えなさい。

[1] 金魚の「軍隊ダンス」はどのような問題を引き起こしていますか？

____

[2] Mr. Fu の金魚マジックとはどんなものか説明しなさい。

____

[3] このマジックについての第 1 の仮説を説明しなさい。

____

[4] 第 2 の仮説を説明しなさい。

____

[5] 第 3 の仮説を説明しなさい。

____

[6] 第 4 の仮説を説明しなさい。

____

[7] 中国の動物の権利団体は金魚にどのようなことがなされていると信じていたのか､具体例を 2 つ書きなさい。

____

____

Notes

[1] in awe 畏怖の念をもって　give rise to ... …を引き起こす　animal-rights 動物の権利
[2] shallow 浅い　unison 調和　line up 整列する　swim laps 往復して泳ぐ　accomplish 達成する　prompt ~ to V ～に V するように促す
[3] speculate 推測する　coat A with B A を B で塗る　filling 詰め物　be distressed ストレスを感じる
[4] fake 偽物の feasible 可能性のある
[5] in synchronization 同調して
[6] contend 主張する　reward 褒美　ridiculous ばかげた
[7] prompt 喚起する　stir up ひきおこす　cruel 残酷な　abuse 虐待する　accusation 非難

2 How are the following hypotheses denied in this passage? Answer in English.

Example: Q: Mr. Fu makes the fish eat iron fillings and uses magnets.

A: *If so, the fish would look distressed, but they don't: they look healthy and well.*

Q1: The gold fish are not real but fake.

A: ______________________________

Q2: Mr. Fu uses a mirror in the water.

A: ______________________________

Q3: Mr. Fu uses hand shadows over the fish to make them move this way and that.

A: ______________________________

Q4: Mr. Fu trained the fish to follow a "leader fish."

A: ______________________________

3 True or False Questions.

1. "Military dance" means that the fish in the tank fight with each other. T F
2. Mr. Fu admits that he uses magnets to do his trick, but he has never explained how he does it. T F
3. The animal rights groups believe that Mr. Fu abuses or is cruel to his fish. T F
4. The animal rights groups complain that the fish look tired after the trick is completed. T F
5. Mr. Fu admits that it would be possible to train fish like dogs. T F
6. Mr. Fu has hinted that he uses electricity to get his fish to perform their dance. T F

Comparison

比べてみよう！

5

エッセイ構成：パラグラフ対照型

❶ トピックの紹介

対照

❷ 比較対象物 A ⟷ ❸ 比較対象物 B

❹ まとめ・コメント

なにか似ているものや事象を二つまたは複数とりあげ、その類似点、相違点を論じていくエッセイパターン。ここでは、比較対象物ＡとＢをそれぞれ別のパラグラフで説明し、比較対照しています。この他に、「類似点」、「相違点」と分けてパラグラフ分けをする方法もあります。その歴史や背景や構成要素など、何か比較基準を設けて、同じレベルで比較をすることが大切です。

A. Macau and Hong Kong

10

1 Why are Macau and Hong Kong enjoying economic freedom, even though both cities belong to China, where communism is still the main economic policy? The answer lies in the cities' complex histories. Both were occupied by Western countries for several centuries, a fact that has made them the most Westernized areas in Asia—and completely different from most of the rest of China. Both cities were returned to China near the end of the twentieth century, but they have been allowed to remain "semi-independent," partly because of their unique culture and partly for the sake of China's economic development, which is quite reliant on them. Both cities have similar histories and enjoy a similar status, but there are some important differences between them. Let's trace the history of each city to see what these differences are.

2 Macau was occupied and colonized by Portugal, making it the first and last European colony in China. Portuguese traders first settled in Macau in the 16th century, and Portugal ruled there until 20 December 1999, when the city was handed back to China. According to China's contract with Portugal, Macau will be allowed to keep a high degree of autonomy until at least 2049, fifty years after the transfer. The main thing that has made the city of Macau so successful is that it is a gambling mecca. Macau's economy is heavily dependent on gambling and tourism. Starting in 1962, the gambling industry was operated under a government-issued monopoly license granted to Stanley Ho, a local tycoon. The monopoly ended in 2002, and several casino owners from Las Vegas attempted to enter the Macau market. Thanks to the millions of Chinese who flock to Macau to gamble at the city's casinos, Macau has prospered and contributed greatly to China's economic growth. It is the only city in China where gambling is officially permitted. Surprisingly, Macau now rakes in more money from gambling than Las Vegas.

3 Now, let's look at the other city, Hong Kong. A city-state situated on China's south coast, Hong Kong was a colony of the British Empire, taken over from China after the First Opium War (1839-42). In 1898, Britain obtained a 99-year lease for Hong Kong from China. Hong Kong was briefly occupied by Japan during World War II, but after the war, the British resumed control until 1997. In 1949, when China became the People's Republic of China under the communist regime, many Chinese fled to Hong Kong fearing persecution by the Communist Party. Hong Kong has thus acted as an asylum for these refugees, as well as for capitalistic corporations. After the communist takeover, many corporations in Shanghai and Guangzhou shifted their operations to Hong Kong. Hong Kong now belongs to China, but in many ways, it has kept its British culture; this is especially true of its educational system, which ensures that most people in Hong Kong speak English. As one of the world's leading financial centers, Hong Kong has a major capitalist service economy characterized by low taxation and free trade. The city's currency, the Hong Kong dollar, is one of the world's strongest trading currencies.

4 Many people see these two cities' situations as highly unique. Under its policy

of "one country, two systems," the Chinese central government is responsible for the territories' defense and foreign affairs, while the two cities maintain their own legal systems, police force, monetary systems, customs practices, and immigration policies. Both cities have prospered economically by taking advantage of their unique position and acting as a bridge between Communist China and the capitalist world. This in turn has helped provide China with financial wealth and economic power. There may be many factors that have led to China's current economic success, but the role of these two cities should not be overlooked or underestimated.

1 左の文章の内容をまとめてみよう。

① 導入 → ② マカオ → ③ 香港 → ④ まとめ

2 Fill in the blanks to summarize each paragraph.

1 In some ways Macau and Hong Kong have had a similar history. Both were colonized by Western countries and now enjoy (e   ) freedom. But there are some differences between them, too.

2 Macau was occupied by (P   ) and returned to China in 1999, but it has been enjoying autonomy under the communist system. Much of its success has come as a result of its being a (g   ) mecca.

3 Hong Kong was colonized by (B   ) and returned to China in 1997, and is now one of the world's leading international (f   ) centers.

4 Under the policy of "one country, (t   ) systems," Macau and Hong Kong maintain a unique position in China.

Notes

1 for the sake of ... …のために　be reliant on ... …に頼っている　trace たどる

2 colonize 植民地化する　be handed back to ... …に返還される　contract 契約　autonomy 自治　transfer 移譲　mecca 中心地　government-issued 政府発行の　monopoly 独占　grant 与える　tycoon 大物実力者　flock to ... …に集まる　prosper 栄える　contribute to ... …に貢献する　rake in money 荒稼ぎする

3 city-state 都市国家　take over 乗っ取る　the First Opium War 第一次アヘン戦争　lease 借地契約　resume 再開する　regime 体制　fled (flee の過去形)逃げる　persecution 迫害　asylum 避難所　refugee 難民　Guangzhou 広州　taxation 課税

4 customs 関税　prosper 繁栄する　take advantage of ... …を利用する　in turn 一方では　over look 看過する

B. Comparison of Right of Succession in the U.K. and Japan

11

1 Since Japan and the U.K. both have a royal family, these two countries' systems are sometimes compared and contrasted. For example, the British Royal Family is more open and allow people outside of royalty to marry into the family, the Japanese Royal Family has a longer lineage of succession, and so on. Here, we'll focus on the differences in succession rights. In Japan, people often ask why women cannot succeed to the throne while in the U.K., many women have become monarchs. But is the British system as open to women as it appears to be?

2 In the U.K., the current system is regulated by the Royal Marriage Act of 1772. Surprisingly, under this act, succession in general is governed by male-preference primogeniture. Sons and their descendants come before daughters and their descendants. Older sons and their descendants come before younger sons. As for the crown itself, at the time of accession, the heir to the throne must be a Protestant (not a Catholic) and enter into communion with the Church of England. Henry VIII established this restriction in the sixteenth century when, because the Catholic religion outlawed divorce, he wanted to divorce his first wife. Elizabeth II, the current monarch, was not expected to become queen when she was born. Her father, George VI was the second son of George V, but George V's first son, Edward VIII, had stepped down from the throne because he wanted to marry Mrs. Simpson, an American and a divorcee, not to mention a Catholic. Thus, when George VI, who had no sons, became King in place of his elder brother, Elizabeth, his first daughter, became next in line for the throne. After George VI died, Elizabeth ascended the throne as Elizabeth II. She has three sons and one daughter. Upon her death or abdication, the throne would go first to Charles, her first son, and then to William, Charles's first son, and then to Henry, Charles's second son. If they for some reason were not available, the throne would go to Andrew, Elizabeth's second son, and then to Andrew's daughters, Beatrice and Eugenie. Following this law, the first son comes first, and then his son and then his daughter, and then the second son ... and so on. Prince William married Catherine ("Kate" Middleton) in 2011, and they had their first son, George, in 2013. Just prior to George's birth, a new law was introduced that stipulated that the first child, whether the second child is a boy or not, would have the right of succession.

3 In Japanese history, Japan has had eight reigning empresses. All of them, however, came to the throne only when there were no eligible brothers, or only as a temporary sovereign to rule in place of the next male successor while he was still young and until he reached an age when he could rule. None of these empresses married or gave birth after ascending to the throne. After the Meiji Restoration, however, Japan imported the Prussian model of imperial succession, in which imperial females were explicitly excluded from any claim to succession. At the same time, in an effort to Westernize and modernize Japan, the Japanese government banned polygamy, which had previously been allowed in any family of noble rank.

Under the Meiji Constitution in 1889, the exclusion of female heirs to the throne was implemented, and the stricture survived after the new constitution was proclaimed in 1947. But in 2006, there was a potential succession crisis, since no male child had been born into the imperial family since Prince Akishino in 1965. Following the birth of Princess Aiko, the only child of the Crown Prince, there was considerable public debate about amending the Imperial House Law to allow female descendants of an emperor to ascend to the throne. But then the Emperor's second son, Akishino, had a son, Hisahito, which put this issue on hold.

4 Both royal families—Japan's and the U.K.'s—need to be modernized, but at the same time, it is a royal family's long history and great traditions that cause it to be respected by the people. This is a contradiction inherent in every royal system. Will both royal families change their succession rights in the future? Should succession be open to anybody, whether a son or a daughter? Or as some people suggest, should the royal system be scrapped altogether?

1 それぞれの段落について、次の質問に答えなさい。

1 第 1 段落で挙げられている、英国王室、日本皇室の違いを説明しなさい。

______

2 イギリス王室継承権について、male-preference primogeniture とはどういうことですか？

______

3 日本の皇室はなぜ継承権から女性を排除することになったのでしょうか？

______

4 王室・皇室を近代化させる際の問題点とは何ですか。

______

Notes

1 lineage 血統　succeed to the throne 王位を継承する　monarch 君主

2 the Royal Marriage Act 王室婚姻法　primogeniture 長子相続法　accession 即位　heir 継承者　enter into communion with ... …の一員となる　the Church of England 英国国教会　outlaw 禁止する　step down 降りる　abdication 退位　stipulate 規定する

3 reigning 君臨する（形容詞）　eligible 適格な　sovereign 君主　explicitly 明白に　polygamy 一夫多妻　implement 実施する　stricture 制限　proclaim 公布する　amend 修正する　put ... on hold …を保留にする

4 inherent 固有の　contradiction 矛盾　inherent ～に固有の　scrap 廃止する

2 Complete the following family tree with the names of kings, queens, princes and princesses.

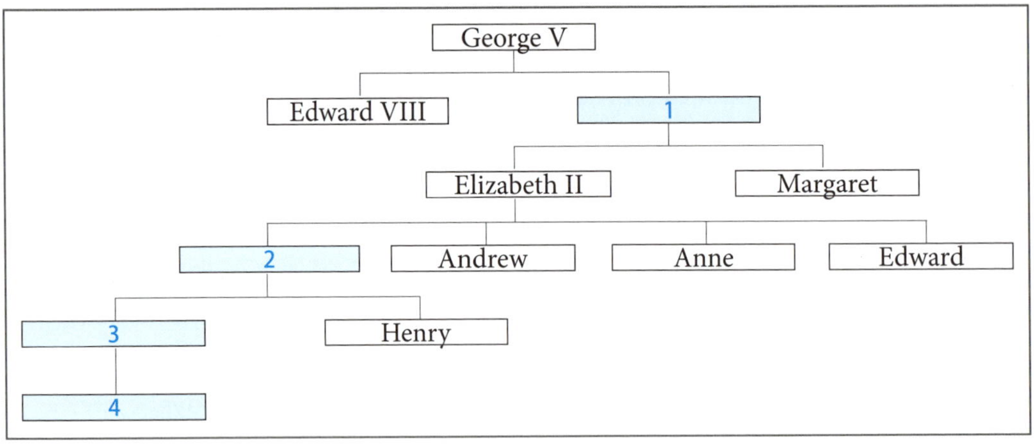

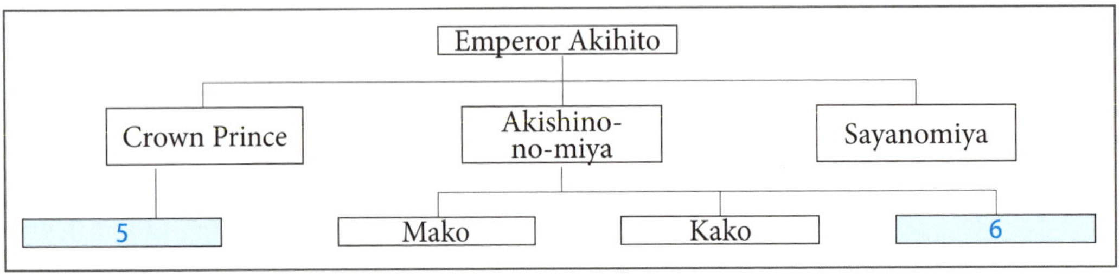

1. __________ 2. __________ 3. __________

4. __________ 5. __________ 6. __________

3 Answer the following questions in English.

1. Why did Henry VIII establish the Church of England?

2. Why did Edward VIII step down from the throne?

3. A new law was recently introduced in the U.K. According to this law, how has the succession order changed?

4. How many reigning empresses has Japan had in its history?

5. When was the exclusion of female heirs regulated in Japan?

6. What was discussed about succession rights in Japan in 2006?

For and Against

賛成と反対

6

エッセイ構成

❶ トピックの紹介
議論をよんでいる問題の紹介

対照

❷ 賛成意見 ⟷ **❸ 反対意見**

❹ まとめ・コメント

現在議論をよんでいる問題をとりあげ、それに賛成する立場からの意見、それに反対する立場からの意見を紹介します。このエッセイパターンの特徴は、ボディとなるパラグラフ同士が対立する関係にあることです。Part 1 の第 1 課(理由で押し切る) は、まずどちらの立場に立つかを明確にし、それを論証するものですが、本課のエッセイパターンは、自分の立場は明確にする必要はなく、客観的に賛成、反対の意見を紹介するものです。

A. Should the Smallpox Virus be Kept?

12

[1] Smallpox is believed to have emerged in human populations in about 10,000 B.C., and has been estimated to have taken the lives of 300-500 million people. In 1796, Edward Jenner developed a smallpox vaccine from a cow, which saved countless lives. Following the Second World War, the WHO (the World Health Organization) started a campaign to eradicate the disease. After smallpox was wiped out, the WHO quickly reached a consensus that existing laboratory stocks of the disease should be destroyed to eliminate the risk of accidental release, and a deadline of 1993 was set for this action. By 1984, stocks from 74 laboratories had been either destroyed or transferred to the two current WHO-sanctioned repositories—in the U.S. and Russia. Many developing countries have long backed the destruction plan. But the WHO has repeatedly pushed back the deadline under pressure from developed countries. Why are we still trying to hold on to such a deadly virus?

[2] Opponents of keeping samples of the virus alive maintain that it poses a constant risk of accidental release, a danger that could have disastrous consequences. They fear that terrorists may steal some smallpox virus stocks and use them as biological warfare to threaten or attack their enemies. If terrorists were to cultivate stocks in large quantities, the potential disaster to the global population is unimaginable. Furthermore, the developing countries are suspicious of Russian and U.S. intentions. They see the research of these two countries, involving the live virus, as a potential threat. Some health officials also question the need, as stated by some supporters of live-virus researchers, to maintain the virus as a means of finding ways to cure AIDS, malaria, tuberculosis, and other infections. There must be other, better ways, these officials say.

[3] On the other hand, supporters of keeping the virus stocks claim that disposal of the smallpox stocks would be a disaster, for several reasons. For one, they say that the world needs these samples in order to develop new drugs to fight the disease should it one day reappear, accidentally or intentionally. As mentioned above, some researchers say that smallpox stocks may also allow them to explore the impact of smallpox on the human immune system, providing insights into other diseases such as AIDS. Also, virus research supporters say that, frightening as it sounds, smallpox samples may already be in the hands of terrorist groups, which weakens the argument that stocks should be destroyed as a way to keep terrorists from obtaining them and using them as weapons. We should keep smallpox stocks, supporters believe, in order to develop ways to neutralize terrorists' biological weapons. As with nuclear weapons, developed countries may hold onto smallpox stocks as a way of maintaining the balance of power. And many scientists also argue that destroying the stocks would actually do little to protect the world from smallpox, since it is now possible to recreate the virus from its genome, which was sequenced in 1994.

4 The WHO once again considered destroying the laboratory stocks in 2007, but it postponed its decision to 2011, and then, in 2011, postponed it again to 2014. The WHO has emphasized that science alone cannot justify retention of this virus, and that any research must have tangible public-health benefits. This issue is, of course, also deeply and unfortunately rooted in power politics.

❶ 左の文章の内容をまとめてみよう。

① 導入（どういう問題か？） → ② 保存に反対の意見

↓

④ 結び ← ③ 保存に賛成の意見

❷ Fill in the blanks to summarize each paragraph.

1 Smallpox virus stocks are now kept only in two countries, the U.S. and (R　　　　　　　). Although the WHO has decided to destroy these viruses, execution of its decision has been frequently postponed.

2 Opponents of keeping the virus fear that stocks of the smallpox virus may be accidentally (r　　　　　　　), causing unimaginable disaster.

3 Supporters say that those stocks are needed to develop new (d　　　　　　　) against smallpox or to fight against biological weapons that use the smallpox virus.

4 This issue is deeply involved in power (p　　　　　　　).

Notes

1 smallpox 天然痘　emerge 出現する　vaccine ワクチン　eradicate 根絶する　wipe out 一掃する　consensus 同意　WHO-sanctioned WHOにより認可された（形容詞）　repository 保管場所　deadly 破壊的な

2 warfare 戦争　cultivate 培養する　be suspicious of ... …を疑う　tuberculosis 結核　infection 感染

3 disposal 廃棄　immune 免疫の　provide insights into ... …に洞察を与える　neutralize ～の効力を失わせる　genome ゲノム　sequence 配列する

4 justify 正当化する　retention 保持　tangible 明白な

B. Was Dropping the Atomic Bombs Right?

13

1 Atomic bombs were dropped on Hiroshima on August 6th, 1945, and on Nagasaki three days later, making Japan the first and (so far) the last country to become the victim of atomic weapons. These days, when people think of "peace," Hiroshima and Nagasaki are often what comes to mind. People around the world have expressed great sympathy with the victims of those atomic bombs and believe it was wrong—immoral—for the American government to use such a dreadful weapon. But given the situation at the time, many people still feel that the U.S. decision was justified. It is well known that great conflict existed among the scientists who were involved in the Manhattan Project (which developed the bombs) over the decision to use the weapons to bring the war to an end. The role of the two atomic bombings in Japan's surrender, and the U.S.'s ethical justification for their use, have been the subject of debate for nearly 70 years.

2 Supporters of the use of the atomic bombs claim, first of all, that those bombs ended the war, which otherwise would have dragged on and on and led to countless more deaths on both sides. At that time, Okinawa was already held by U.S. forces, who were set to invade the mainland of Japan. But the Americans on Okinawa were suffering from the Japanese army's perseverance and the resistance of the islands' civilians, since most Japanese people had been taught to believe that it would be better to die than to surrender to their enemy. People were encouraged to fight to the death, or, if about to be captured or defeated, to commit suicide. According to some estimates, if the war had continued, Americans would have suffered one million additional casualties, while Japanese would have suffered many, many millions. "Kamikaze attacks (suicide attacks)" terrified the Americans. The damage to Japan was devastating, and the country was on the brink of defeat, but the chief commanders of the Japanese army were showing that they would never surrender. Supporters of the use of atomic bombs thus believed that it would be the only way to stop the war and minimize the number of casualties.

3 Furthermore, some supporters argue that if the bombs had not been dropped, the Soviet Union would have invaded and taken over Japan. If this had happened, Japan, under a communist government, would never have enjoyed the economic prosperity it has over the last seven decades.

4 On the other hand, there are those who believe it was wrong for the Americans to use atomic bombs to stop the war. The bombings were unnecessary, they say. The war was all but over, and Japan would have been forced to surrender in a very short time anyway. Even ex-president Herbert Hoover and some U.S. military leaders believed this to be the case. The sea around Japan was already blocked and Okinawa was occupied, which meant that U.S. forces could freely invade Honshu. Meanwhile Germany, Japan's ally, had already surrendered several months earlier. Some historians argue that the reason why the U.S. decided to use the atomic bombs,

although it knew the end of the war was in sight, was that it expected to be the new world leader and wanted to show off its power. At that time, the U.S. was convinced that the Soviet Union would be its future rival. In other words, it was sheer political calculation that made the U.S. decide to use atomic bombs.

5 At the same time, many people oppose the use of the atomic bombs on different grounds. They say that not only the short-term but also the long-term aftermath of the use of such weapons should have been considered. As is well known, the atomic bombs at Hiroshima and Nagasaki have affected millions who were not directly involved in the war. Fallout from the bombs has had a lasting effect on the innocent offspring of the victims.

6 An international law established at the Hague Convention of 1907 mentions a distinction between "targeted area bombardment" and "indiscriminate area bombardment," and a distinction between a defended and an undefended city. According to international laws that existed at the time of the use of the atomic bombs on Japan, America's action should have been illegal. The question of whether the two atomic bombs saved more people than they killed may never be answered.

1 それぞれの段落について、次の質問に答えなさい。

1 このエッセイでは何が討論されているか？

____

2 原爆投下についての擁護論を、犠牲者の数の点から述べなさい。

____

3 原爆投下についての擁護論を、政治的な点から述べなさい。

____

4 原爆投下に反対する第1の理由は何ですか？

____

5 原爆投下に反対する第2の理由は何ですか？

____

6 1907年のハーグ会議で決められたこととは？

____

Notes

1 sympathy 同情 given the situation at the time 当時の状況を考えれば bring A to an end Aを終わらせる surrender 降伏 ethical 倫理的な justification 正当化 2 drag on 長引く perseverance 忍耐力 capture 捕らえる casualty 犠牲者 devastating 破壊的な on the brink of ... …に瀕して commander 指揮官 minimize 最小化する 3 prosperity 繁栄 4 all but ほぼ ally 同盟国 show off 見せつける sheer 全く 5 aftermath 結果 fallout 放射能灰 offspring 子孫 6 bombardment 爆撃 indiscriminate 無差別の

2 Choose the two statements that are NOT mentioned as a reason for using an atomic bomb.

(　　) (　　)

a. U.S. forces couldn't land on Okinawa for political reasons.
b. Japanese people might not have surrendered for any reason.
c. Japanese forces were afraid of kamikaze attacks.
d. The leaders of the Japanese army insisted on continuing the war against the U.S.
e. The Soviet Union had ambitions to occupy Japan.
f. To use atomic bombs would minimize the number of victims both for Japan and the U.S.

3 Answer the following questions in English.

1. What did Herbert Hoover and some U.S. military leaders believe about the state of Japan just before the end of the war?

____

2. Which country surrendered first, Germany or Japan?

____

3. Which country did the U.S. believe would be its rival in the years following the war?

____

4. What does "the aftermath of the use of weapons" mean in the context of this essay?

____

Classification

分類してみよう！

7

エッセイ構成：パラグラフ対照型

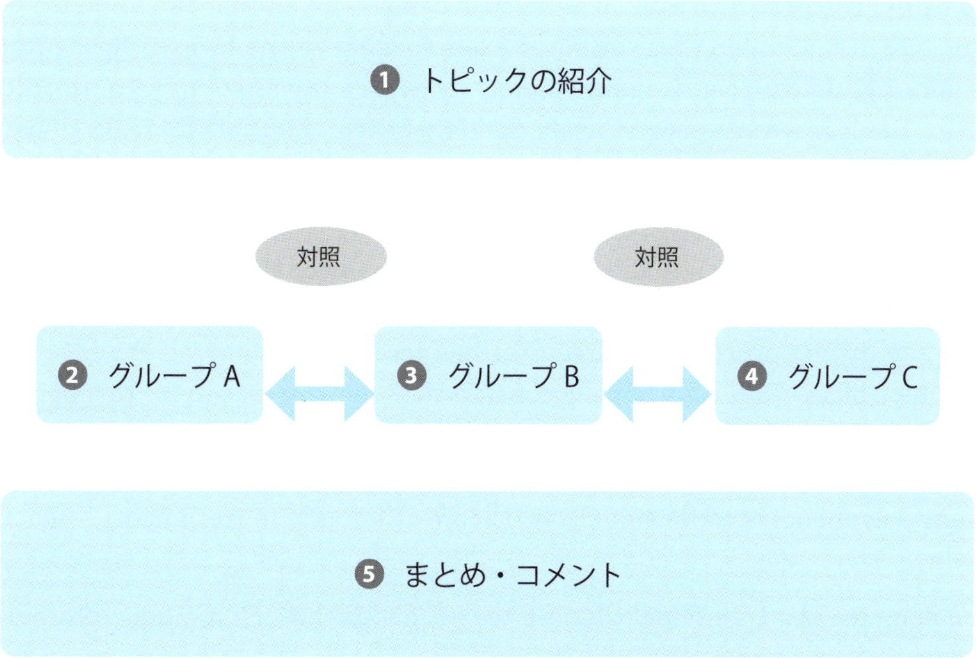

ある基準を設け、その基準に従って、何かをいくつかのグループに分類するエッセイパターンです。どういう基準で分類するのかをまずはっきりさせます。それから構成要素をそれぞれのグループに振り分けていきます。ボディとなる各パラグラフがそれぞれ対照となっていることに注目してください。

A. Tea

14

1 Teas can generally be divided into six categories based on how they are processed: white, yellow, green, oolong, black, and post-fermented teas. Among these, green tea, oolong tea, and black tea are the most popular and most commonly found in the market. Tea plants are native to East and South Asia, which was a major reason that European powers colonized these areas. There is a funny story about how black tea became black tea. When Europeans started transporting tea from India to Europe, the green tea often turned black because of the heat in the ships as they sailed across the Indian Ocean. This story is partly true, in that the same tea leaves become green tea, oolong tea, or black tea according to the level of fermentation. After picking, unless they are immediately dried, tea leaves soon begin to wilt and oxidize. The leaves turn progressively darker as their chlorophyll breaks down and tannins are released. This enzymatic oxidation process is called fermentation, which is what took place on those long-ago ships.

2 Green tea, which originates in China and has become associated with many cultures throughout Asia, is made from tea leaves that have undergone minimal oxidization during processing. Green tea has recently become "all the rage" in the West, where black tea is traditionally consumed. The main reason for this popularity has to do with health: many studies have found that regular green tea drinkers may have a lower risk of developing heart disease and certain types of cancer. Green tea contains polyphenols and flavonoids, which are also found in fresh fruits, vegetables, and wine.

3 Oolong tea is a traditional Chinese tea produced through a unique process that includes withering under a hot direct sun and oxidation before curling and twisting. The degree of fermentation can range from 8% to 85%, depending on the variety and production style. This tea category is especially popular in South China and Southeast Asia. The name "oolong" came into the English language from the Chinese name, which means "black dragon." It's believed that drinking oolong tea just after eating (especially beef and pork) can reduce the amount of fat absorbed into the body.

4 Black tea is more thoroughly oxidized than oolong and green teas, and is generally stronger in flavor. In the Chinese and Japanese languages, black tea is known as "red tea," because when the tea is served it looks red. The Western term "black tea" refers to the color of the oxidized leaves. While green tea usually loses its flavor within a year, black tea retains its flavor for several years. According to one study, black tea consumption reduces the risk of coronary artery disease. A German study, however, shows that the addition of milk actually blocks the vascular protective effects of tea.

5 Tea is now an essential commodity for billions of people all over the world. In fact, it is difficult to imagine life today without tea in its many forms.

❶ この文章をまとめてみよう。

① 導入（結論）
(　　　　　　)の度合いによって茶は 3 種類に分けられる。

→ ② 緑茶

→ ③ 烏龍茶

→ ④ 紅茶

→ ⑤ 結び

❷ Fill in the blanks to summarize each paragraph.

1 There are many tea types, with their differences based on how they are (p　　　　　　).

2 Green tea comes from leaves that have undergone minimal (o　　　　　　). This tea contains polyphenols and flavonoids, and is thus becoming popular for (h　　　　　　) reasons.

3 Oolong tea is produced through a process of fermentation that ranges from 8% to 85% fermentation. This tea is said to reduce the absorption of (f　　　　　　) in the body after eating.

4 Black tea, the most oxidized of the three tea types, is stronger in (f　　　　　　) than the other teas and is believed to reduce the risk of coronary artery disease.

5 Tea is now (e　　　　　　) in the daily lives of people all over the globe.

Notes

1 process 加工する　post-fermented 発酵後の　be native to ~ ～原産である　European powers ヨーロッパ列強　fermentation 発酵　wilt しおれる　oxidize 酸化する　progressively 次第に　chlorophyll 葉緑素　tannin タンニン　enzymatic 酵素の　oxidation 酸化
2 oxidization 酸化　all the rage 大人気　polyphenol ポリフェノール　flavonoid フラボノイド
3 wither しおれる　curling 曲がること　twisting よじれること
4 thoroughly 完全に　coronary artery 冠状動脈　vascular 血管の
5 commodity 日用品

B. Folk Tales

1 Every country has its own folk tales. These tales have been handed down from generation to generation, at first orally, and then, eventually, they were written down and preserved in some form or other. Folk tales can be categorized into four types: myths, legends, fables, and fairy tales. Do you know the differences among these four kinds of folk tales? Let's take a quick look.

2 A myth is usually a sacred narrative tale that explains how the world began and how humankind appeared in it. The best-known examples of this category are, of course, the Greek myths, with their pantheon of gods and goddesses. In many cases, myths feature supernatural characters who are somehow involved with the origins and lives of humans. As for the Greek myths, the gods and goddesses were closely linked to and interacted in both positive and negative ways with Greek people. Many myths are about the formation of a particular nation and suggest that its origins are sacred—that the nation's people's ancestors were gods. In many cases throughout history, rulers have used myths as the source of their power, claiming that they are direct descendants of gods. The emperors of Japan, for example, were long believed to be descendants of the gods found in Japanese mythology.

3 A legend is a narrative tale about human actions related to a historical time or event. In general, while myths belong to a certain country or people, legends deal with more local events and people. Of course, some legends are about heroes or heroines who are believed to have built a nation. But such heroes and heroines are usually more human than the god-like characters in myths. A legend lies somewhere between reality and imagination, fact and fiction, history and storytelling. It is based on real events or people, but the reality over time takes on fictional narrative elements. By studying legends, we can to a certain extent get an idea of how people in the past lived and thought.

4 A fable is very often disguised reality, usually with animals standing in for people. There is often a moral lesson woven into the story, for children and sometimes for adults. The Western fable tradition began with the short moral tales ascribed to Aesop. He was a slave in Greece, who collected and wrote many short stories, with animals as the main characters. His stories are said to have been based on Ancient Indian stories. The literary and religious traditions of China and Japan also include fables. The animals, supernatural creatures, plants and so on that are a fable's characters focus in on some truth about human beings and society.

5 Our last type of folk tale, the fairy tale, is a short story that features fantastic characters such as fairies, elves, giants, witches, mermaids, and so on. While legends are closely related to certain local places, fairy tales are more universal, without local or national boundaries. Many cultures' stories have similar plots and themes. These stories often involve magic, curses, spells, and so on. "Cinderella," "Snow White,"

and "Beauty and the Beast" are good examples. The Grimm Brothers' fairy tales are perhaps the best known. The Grimms collected the fantastic stories they heard as they traveled around rural Germany. Many fairy tales end happily, hence the expression "fairy-tale ending," but some stories do not. Some fairy tales depict cruel scenes and actions, which some psychologists claim is the fairy tale's way of teaching us about human nature (both good and bad). In many cases, though, the dark side of fairy tales has been changed to make them less frightening, so that children can read them without being scared. Psychologists contend that fairy tales are a good source for the study of the human subconscience. Hans Christian Andersen later made fairy tales into a sophisticated literary art form.

6 It is sometimes difficult to decide which genre a particular story belongs to. Reading a story, and trying to decide whether it is a myth, a legend, or a fairy tale can add to the story's fun.

1 それぞれの段落について、次の質問に答えなさい。

1 民話はどのようにして継承されますか？

____

2 神話の特徴を簡潔にまとめなさい。

____

3 伝説の特徴を簡潔にまとめなさい。

____

4 寓話の特徴を簡潔にまとめなさい。

____

5 おとぎ話の特徴を簡潔にまとめなさい。

____

6 この分類分けで難しいこととは？

____

Notes

1 orally 口頭で eventually 最後には fable 寓話
2 sacred 神にまつわる(形容詞) narrative 物語の pantheon パンテオン・神殿 feature 登場させる
3 fictional 作り話の to a certain extent ある程度
4 disguised 偽装された stand in for ... …の代わりをする woven (weave の過去分詞)織る be ascribed to ... …に帰する focus in on ... …に焦点をあてる
5 feature 登場させる elf 小人 curse 呪い spell 呪文 hence それ故 depict 描く cruel 残酷な contend 主張する subconscience 潜在意識 sophisticated 洗練された
6 genre ジャンル particular 特定の add to 増大させる

❷ If the statement is related to "myth," write **M**, "legend," write **L**, "fable," write **F**, or "fairy tale," write "**FT**."

1. These stories are related to gods and goddesses. ( )
2. These stories sometimes tell of the origins of a certain nation. ( )
3. These stories usually end happily. ( )
4. It is sometimes said that some of these stories show what goes on in people's deep mind. ( )
5. In these stories, animals think and speak. ( )
6. Some of the original forms of these stories were too terrifying for young children to read. ( )
7. These stories are very often used to teach children moral lessons. ( )
8. Hans Christian Anderson turned these stories into "literature." ( )
9. Such stories are sometimes used to justify the power of kings or emperors. ( )
10. These stories show heroes and heroines who are usually half real and half imaginary. ( )

❸ Fill in the blanks.

1. A myth very often claims that the original ancestors of a certain people were ( ).
2. A legend usually refers to ( ) rather than national events or people.
3. Aesop, who was a ( ) in Greece, is said to be the "father" of fables.
4. The Grimm Brothers collected folk tales from all around ( ).
5. Characters in legends are more ( ) than those in myths.

TRY

Write your own Essay!!

つぎのタイトルでエッセイの構成を考えてみよう。

この課で扱ったエッセイ構造を使って、自分でエッセイ構造を考えてみよう。次のエッセイタイトルを使って簡単にエッセイ構造を考え、ポイントを日本語で書いてみよう。余裕があればそれを英文のエッセイにしてみよう。

4 Several Explanations

1. 日本人のルーツは？
   Where did Japanese people come from?
2. なぜ恐竜は絶滅したのか？
   What led to the extinction of the dinosaurs?

5 Comparisons

1. 日本人とアメリカ人を比較する。
   Compare the Japanese national character with the American national character.
2. 猫好きと犬好きを比較する。
   Compare "cat lovers" with "dog lovers."
3. 電子書籍と印刷書籍を比較する。
   Compare e-book reading with print reading.

6 For and Against

1. 学校の９月入学制に賛成・反対
   What would be the benefits and drawbacks of starting Japan's school year in fall?
2. サマータイム制導入に賛成・反対
   What would be the benefits and drawbacks of starting daylight saving time (summer time) in Japan?
3. 日本語の書法のローマ字化に賛成・反対
   What would be the benefits and drawbacks of romanizing Japan's writing system?

7 Classification

1. 小説の分類
   What are the different novel types (genres)?
2. 現代のポピュラー音楽の分類
   What are the different types of popular music today?

Part III

エッセイ構成：フロー型

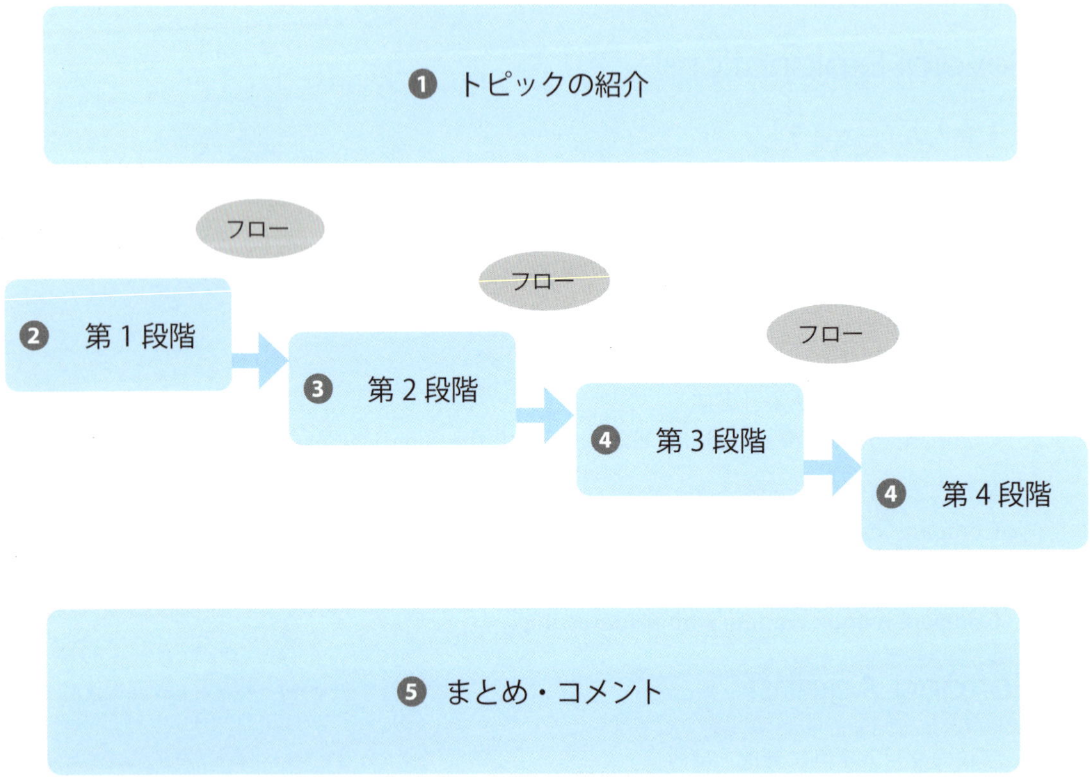

Part III のエッセイパターンは、ボディとなるパラグラフを時間の経過の順に並べていくものです。何かの歴史を説明していく、何かの作業のプロセスを追っていく、何かの事象を述べ、それがもたらした結果を述べる、などのトピックを扱います。時系列に沿って述べていくエッセイパターンは、マニュアル、履歴書、何かの歴史を書く際によく使われます。

History
歴史をたどる

8

エッセイ構成：フロー型

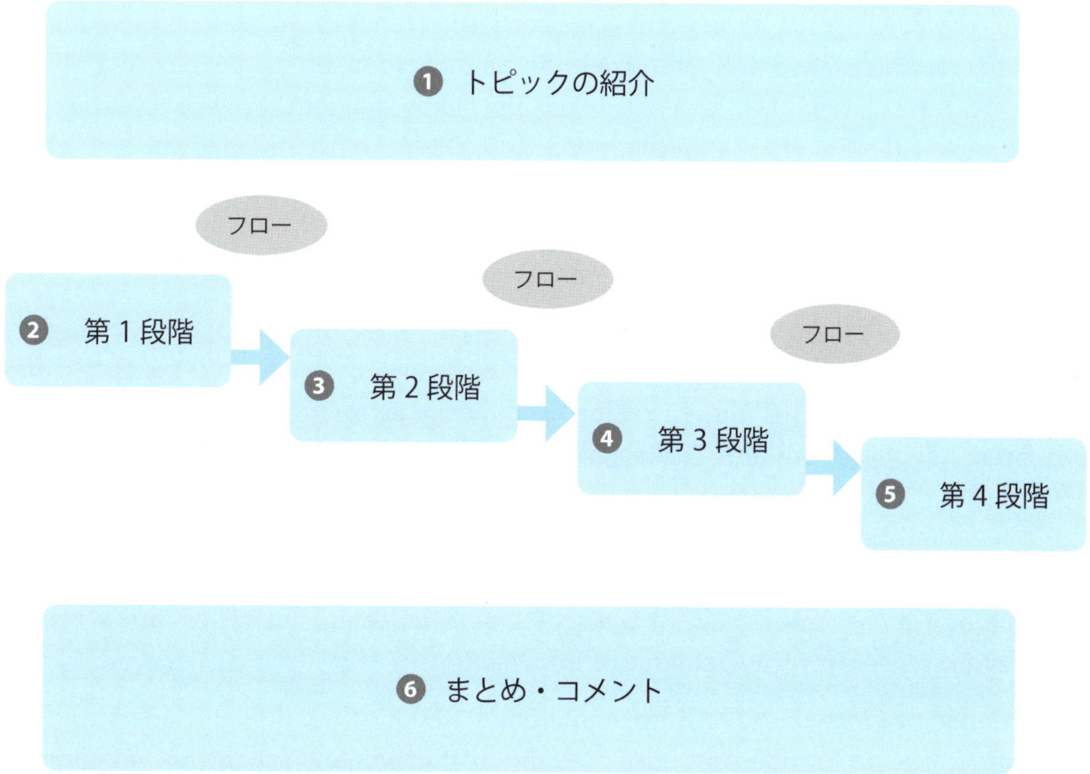

あるトピックについて、その時間的変遷を追っていくもの。まず何の歴史について説明するのかから始まり、時間的に早い内容から歴史をたどっていきます。最終段階として、現在の状態で終わる。「まとめ」のパラグラフでは、現在の問題点、もしくは未来の予測などが述べられる。このエッセイパターンの特徴は、いくつかあるボディが時間の流れに沿って並べられていることである。

A. History of Coffee

16

1 It is common knowledge that tea has played an important role in and even changed world history. But coffee has also played a decisive role, and knowing the history of coffee can help us better understand some important aspects of global history.

2 The name "coffee" is thought to have come from the language of the Kingdom of Kaffa in Ethiopia, where the first coffee plants were grown. Of the many stories that are told about how people discovered coffee, the following is probably the most famous. One day, a man called Kaldi, a goat-herd, saw his goats eating some red berries and becoming so excited! Kaldi wondered if the berries had some special power, so he tried them himself. He, too, became excited and energized. So he took some of the berries to a Muslim monastery and showed them to a holy man. The monk thought they were evil, and threw them into a fire. But then, a lovely aroma arose from the fire. Intrigued, some monks picked out the roasted beans and ground them up, then dissolved the powder in hot water. This, says the legend, was the world's very first cup of coffee. From then on, coffee began to be used in monasteries to keep the monks awake during their long prayers.

3 Around 1,000 A.D., Arab traders discovered coffee in Ethiopia and brought it back to their country, where they started to cultivate it. By the 15th century, coffee was being grown in the Yemeni region, and by the sixteenth century it was known in Persia, Egypt, Syria, and Turkey, all of which opened coffee shops. There was a particular reason why coffee became so popular among Muslim people. Alcoholic drinks are prohibited by the Koran, the holy book of Islam, so people used coffee's mysterious powers to energize themselves, drinking it as a substitute for alcohol. Coffee houses became excellent places for various social activities and served as important centers for the exchange of information.

4 Coffee was introduced to Europe in around 1,600. It was Italian traders who first brought coffee to Europe, and once they did, it immediately caught on. At first, the Christian Church was suspicious of coffee, calling it the "bitter invention of Satan." Christians regarded coffee as the "beverage of Muslims" and urged the Pope to ban its consumption. Pope Clement VIII, however, was enchanted by this exotic beverage and decided to accept it. To the people's surprise, he "baptized" coffee instead of banning it, enabling Christians to enjoy this Muslim drink, too. Coffee soon spread all over Europe.

5 In the mid-1600s, it arrived in America. At that time, tea was Americans' favorite drink, following the custom of their European forefathers. But the American colonists didn't like the way the King of England imposed heavy taxes on tea imported from England. So they revolted, which led to the Boston Tea Party, in which hundreds of barrels of tea imported from England were tossed into the sea. From then on, Americans switched from tea to coffee and began to cultivate coffee domestically, leading to the development of large coffee farms called plantations that used African slaves as workers. In America, coffee—like cotton—has always been deeply connected to black slavery.

6 In 1901, the first "instant" coffee was invented by a Japanese-American chemist. In 1938, the Nestlé Company in Switzerland invented freeze-dried coffee. In 1971 Starbucks opened its first store in Seattle and now has thousands of shops around the globe. Coffee is now a truly international drink.

1 この文章をまとめてみよう。

① 導入
(　　　　　　)の歴史について述べる。
→ ② 第1段階（始まり）
→ ③ 第2段階
↓ ④ 第3段階
← ⑤ 第4段階
↓ ⑥ 現在の状態

2 Fill in the blanks to summarize each paragraph.

1 Like tea, coffee has played an important role in world (h　　　　　　).

2 Coffee originally came from (E　　　　　　), and it is said that a goat-herd discovered the energizing power of coffee and took it to a (m　　　　　　), where it became popular.

3 Coffee was brought to the Arab countries and soon became popular among (M　　　　　　), because (a　　　　　　) drinks were prohibited by the Koran.

4 Around 1600, coffee was introduced to Europe, but because it was believed to be the "beverage of (M　　　　　　)," it was about to be prohibited when (P　　　　　　) Clement VIII decided to accept it.

5 Coffee was brought to America, where Americans started to cultivate coffee plants using black (s　　　　　　).

6 Coffee is now an (i　　　　　　) drink.

Notes

1 decisive 決定的な　aspect 側面　2 goat-herd ヤギ番　become energized 元気になる　monastery 修道院　intrigued 不思議に思って　ground (grind の過去形)挽く　prayer 祈り　3 cultivate 栽培する　Yemeni イエーメンの　prohibit 禁止する　substitute 代替物　4 catch on 人気を得る　be suspicious of ... …に懐疑的である　Satan 悪魔　beverage 飲み物　urge ~ to V ～に V するようせかす　ban 禁止する　consumption 消費　Pope 法皇　be enchanted by ... …に魅了される　exotic 異国の　baptize 洗礼させる　5 forefather 先駆者　revolt 反乱を起こす　barrel バレル(石油の量の単位)　toss 放り上げる　domestically 国内で

B. History of the Weekend

17

[1] It is common practice in many countries to take Sunday off from work, and taking both Sunday and Saturday off has recently become even more common. Have you ever asked yourself why there are seven days in a week, and why we have Sunday and Saturday off?

[2] In English, a day when you don't have to work is called a "holiday," which originally meant a "holy day." For many centuries, Sunday has been a holy day or day of rest in the Western world. This idea derives from the Christian Bible. When God created the world, he is said to have worked six days and rested on the seventh. Later, when he revealed the "Ten Commandments" to Moses, God told people to keep one day a week as a day of rest. Thus, the idea of taking the seventh day—Sunday—off from work has been the convention in Western society for a long time, and is now the norm all over the world. The Catholic Church for a long time prohibited any work on "holy" Sunday to allow Catholics to concentrate on serving God by taking part in "holy" activities such as going to church, singing hymns, and reading the Bible.

[3] This "keeping Sunday holy" aspect of Christian teaching became especially prominent in some areas of the United States, where, in the 18th and 19th centuries, there were strict religious observances. These religious laws, called "Blue Laws," prohibited stores from doing business on Sunday and restricted leisure activities on that "holy day." Even today, some small shops are closed on Sunday in certain strict Christian areas.

[4] In the Western world, the one-day-off-a-week system was the norm for many centuries. The move towards the two-day weekend is relatively recent. In America, working hours began to be gradually reduced from before the Civil War and up to the turn of the 20th century. During that time, working only a half day on Saturday became acceptable and eventually standard practice. While it took many centuries to change over to one and a half days off, it only took a comparatively few years for the custom of a full two-day weekend to evolve. This change was in response to the demands of the labor unions, who called for the two-day weekend to satisfy Jewish workers, for whom Saturday is the "holy day" (they call it the "Sabbath"), not Sunday. For Islamic people, Friday was and is the "holy day." In 1926, Henry Ford began shutting down his automobile factories for all of Saturday and Sunday. In 1929, the Amalgamated Clothing Workers of America became the first labor union to succeed in securing a two-day weekend. After that, most American companies gradually followed. In 1938, President Franklin Roosevelt signed the Fair Labor Standards Act, which established a five-day, 40-hour work week for many workers.

[5] This five-day work week produced many economic by-products. The weekend was no longer just a time for serving God or for relaxing and taking part in limited holiday activities. It became busy. New entertainment and leisure businesses suddenly

emerged such as cinemas, sports, going for drives, and dining out. Such activities became common pastimes for people and stimulated the national economy. Although working hours were reduced, people worked harder to make up for the loss and to finance their weekend leisure activities. This trend quickly spread throughout Europe.

6 The two-day weekend has become the norm in many places across the world, because with each country's economy linked to the global economy, if you have a different work-week system, you will lose many business opportunities and be put in an inconvenient position. In Japan, many companies and schools now operate under the two-day weekend system, which became common between the years 1980 and 2000. Before then, most workers in Japan worked full-time from Monday to Friday, and half-time on Saturday. (This half-time Saturday came to be called "Han don," meaning half-holiday: "don" came from the Dutch word Zondag, meaning Sunday. "Hakata Dontaku" is also derived from this word, Zondag.) In the Edo period, Japanese rarely had a holiday (usually only "Bon" and New Year's). The weekend system, along with many other Westernizing and modernizing changes, entered Japan during the Meiji Era.

1 それぞれの段落について、次の質問に答えなさい。

1 週休１日制と週休２日制はどちらの方が歴史が古いですか？

____

2 日曜日を聖なる日とすべきという考えのもとに、カトリック教会が日曜日に働くことを禁止したのはどうしてですか？

____

3 "Blue Laws" とはどんな法律か説明しなさい。

____

4 アメリカで、週休２日制への移行はユダヤ教徒への配慮であると述べられていますが、それはなぜですか？

____

5 週休２日制によって繁栄した娯楽産業とは？

____

6 世界中が週休２日制に移行しているのはなぜですか？

____

Notes

2 derive from ... …に由来する　reveal 知らせる　Ten Commandments 十戒　Moses モーゼ　convention 慣習　norm 規範　hymn 賛美歌　3 prominent 顕著な　observance 慣習　4 the Civil War 南北戦争　comparatively 比較的に　evolve 進化する　Sabbath 安息日　the Amalgamated Clothing Workers of America 米国合同繊維労働組合　the Fair Labor Standards Act 公正労働基準法　5 by-product 副産物　emerge 出現する　pastime 余暇　stimulate 刺激する　make up for ... …を補う　finance 資金を作る　6 be derived from ... …起源である　Dutch オランダの

❷ Answer the following questions in English.

1. In the Bible's Old Testament, why is Sunday a special day?

____

2. How did the Catholic Church respond to the idea that Sunday was a holy day?

____

3. In the U.S., in what areas are some shops still closed on Sunday?

____

4. Which day is a holiday for Muslims?

____

5. Which American labor union was the first to give workers a full two-day weekend?

____

6. In Japan's Edo Era, what were the only holidays or days off work?

____

❸ Write *T* if the sentence is true, *F* if it is false.

1. It took far longer to change from a one-day weekend to a one-and-a-half-day weekend than it did to change from a one-and-a-half-day weekend to a two-day weekend. T F

2. The "Sabbath" is an Islamic holiday that is equivalent to Sunday in the Christian world. T F

3. The Japanese expression "Han don" used for Saturday comes from the word "Bon," which means a half holiday. T F

Process
過程を説明する
9

エッセイの構成：フロー型

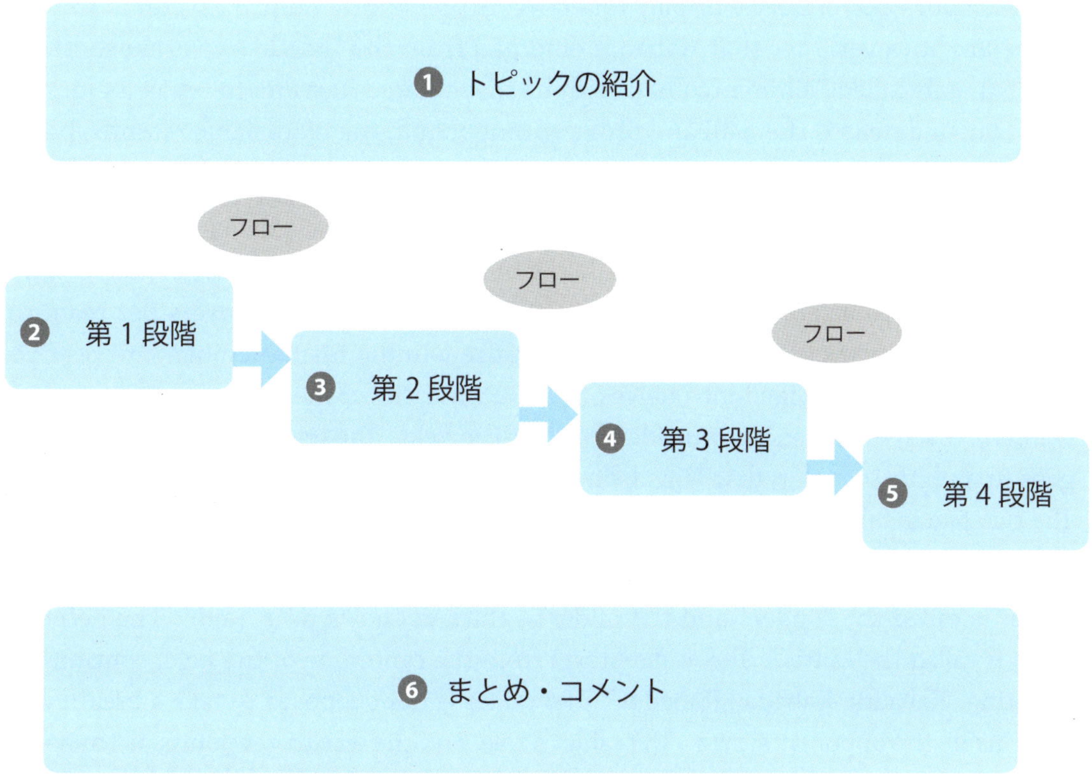

何かの過程を説明します。導入で何の過程を説明するのかを明示し、そのあとでその過程を説明していきます。「始めに→次に→それから→最後に」と進んでいくエッセイパターンです。ここではスポーツの試合の流れとアメリカの大統領選挙の流れを説明していきます。複雑なプロセスでもひとつひとつていねいに説明していくことで流れをつかむことができます。

A. How to Play Kabaddi

18

1 Kabaddi is a sport that is played and enjoyed in some countries, but that is not popular among Japanese, though you may have read about it or watched it being played on TV. Compared with most other sports, Kabaddi comes across as strange and unique, though some say it resembles wrestling and rugby. Kabaddi originated in India, perhaps as early as 4,000 years ago. According to one historian, the sport may have developed during prehistoric times when people had to defend themselves from sudden attacks from wild beasts. Men formed groups to counter-attack the animals, and Kabaddi's current style of play reflects this prehistoric hunting system. Another historian, however, says that Kabaddi emerged from the "Battle of Kurakushetra" in which a man called Abhimanyu had to fight seven fierce warriors to break a blockade. Abhimanyu defeated them all and broke through, and, the historian contends, people invented this game and started to play it as a way to commemorate this battle.

2 How is Kabaddi played and what are its rules? A game proceeds like this. It is normally played for 40 minutes with a break of five or ten minutes in the middle. First, you need 24 people split into two teams of twelve. Only seven players per team can be on the playing field at the same time. The remaining team members are reserves. The playing field is divided into halves (10m×13m each for men and 8m×12m each for women). Each team has its own side or end of the field. The teams flip a coin to see who goes first, with the team that wins being on "offense" and the other team on "defense." The two teams take turns being on offense and defense until the game is over.

3 The offensive team sends out one player to the opponents' side of the field. This player is called the "raider," and the raider's attack is known as a "raid." The defensive team is called the "antis." The raider starts from the centerline of the field, continuously shouting "Kabaddi, Kabaddi, Kabaddi." The raider is not supposed to take a breath while he is inside the opponents' area. The raider's role, and the way to get points, is to see how many opponents he/she can touch on the hand or leg while he/she is in the defense's area. The "antis" touched by the raider during the attack are declared "out," and have to leave the field. The raider has to return to his own area after touching as many opponents as possible and must do all this while shouting "Kabaddi ..." in one long, continuous breath.

4 When the raider comes back to his own side of the field, the number of people he/she has touched equals the number of points the team gets. And then the next raider goes to the opponents' side of the field. If a team gets all the opponents "out," that team gets two points as a bonus, which is called a "Lona."

5 The "antis," meanwhile, have to catch the raider before he returns to his own area, and must try to hold the raider so that he can't continue to chant "Kabaddi." If he/she stops chanting, he/she is "cut." The defenders are called "stoppers." Each team can have only four stoppers on the field, and only one stopper can try to stop a raider at any given time.

[6] Considering that Kabaddi is so popular in India and some other countries, don't you think it is worth trying?

1 この文章をまとめてみよう。

① 導入 カバディの歴史 → ② どうやって試合が始まるか？ → ③ どのように試合を進めるか？

↓

④ どのようにして点数は入るか？ → ⑤ 防御側はどうやって攻撃を防ぐか？ → ⑥ まとめ

2 Fill in the blanks to summarize each paragraph.

[1] Although few people know about it in Japan, Kabaddi is popular in some countries. Some say that Kabaddi developed from a prehistoric (h) system, and some say that it emerged to commemorate a famous (b) in which a brave man managed to break a blockade of enemies.

[2] 24 people are played in (t) teams in a Kabaddi game and the game lasts 40 minutes. (S) players per team can play on the playing field which is (d) into two. A game starts by (f) a coin to decide which team is on offense and which team is on (d).

[3] The offensive team sends the "raider" to the opponents' side. The raider has to continue to (s) "Kabaddi, Kabaddi, Kabaddi, without taking (b) and has to touch as many (o) as possible.

[4] The number of opponents the raiders touch equals the number of (p) the offensive team gets. If the raiders touch all the opponents, the offensive team gets a (b) called a "Lona".

[5] The "antis" have to catch the raider and each team can have one (s) out of four on the field.

Notes

[1] come across as ... …という印象を与える　counter-attack ～に反撃する　fierce 荒々しい　blockade 封鎖　contend 主張する　commemorate ～を記念する
[2] reserve 補欠　flip 指ではじく　take turns 交代に行う
[4] equal ～にあたる
[5] at any given time いついかなる時でも

B. How to Select an American President

19

1 Every four years, in the same year as the summer Olympic Games, the United States has a big event—the Presidential election. Because the U.S. exerts such an outsized influence on global affairs, "Who will be the American President?" is always a big topic, not only inside the U.S. but around the world. Roughly speaking, the difference between the U.S. President and the British or Japanese Prime Minister is that the former is elected directly by the people while the latter is elected indirectly through Members of Parliament. The American presidential election process is, however, quite complicated and hard to understand for outsiders. How is the election carried out?

2 First, let's take a look at who is eligible to be a U.S. president. According to the U.S. Constitution, the president should be a natural-born citizen of the U.S., at least thirty-five-years old, and must have been a permanent resident in the U.S. for at least fourteen consecutive years. No person can be elected president for more than two four-year terms of office. (One exception was Franklin Roosevelt who stayed on for a third and then fourth term during the crisis of World War II.)

3 The first step in electing a president is to choose a candidate from each political party. At the local level, people who support the same party choose their candidate, either through an election (called a primary) or through discussion (caucuses). These local elections are held between January and June of the election year. Then, at the national level, usually in July or early August, each party holds a nominating convention and chooses one candidate from those chosen at the local level. The party's presidential candidate then chooses a vice-president candidate.

4 The real presidential election starts after the convention, usually in September. The two sets of nominees—the presidential and vice-presidential nominees of the Republican Party and the Democratic Party—appear on TV and give speeches and engage in debates to encourage people to vote for them. The nominees explain their views and policies, often attacking those of their rivals. Other parties can offer candidates, too, but in reality it is only these two parties' candidates who compete against each other and have a chance of winning.

5 Then the voting starts. On the first Tuesday after the first Monday in November, registered voters go to the polls to vote for the presidential candidate of their choice. The votes are counted, and this is called the "popular vote." But the election is not over yet. Each state has a certain number of "electors" according to its population size. The presidential candidate who wins the popular vote in each state gets all of the electoral votes for that state. So, if one state has 30 electors and the candidate for the Democratic Party wins the popular vote for that state, he/she receives all 30 of the state's electoral votes. Whether the Democratic Party wins 999:1001, or 1:1999, the Democratic Party wins 30 electors. This system is called "winner-take-all

system." When all the electoral votes are counted in Congress, the candidate with the most votes becomes president. There are 538 electoral votes: to win, the candidate must receive at least a majority of these votes—270.

6 The new President starts his job at noon on January 20 of the following year. This date is known as Inauguration Day, and the new President has to take the presidential oath and then makes a speech outlining his/her vision for his administration for the coming four years.

❶ それぞれの段落について、次の質問に答えなさい。

1 大統領制と首相制の違いを説明しなさい。

____

2 アメリカ大統領選挙に出ることができる資格を挙げなさい。

____

3 地方レベルで候補者を選ぶ際の２つのやり方を挙げなさい。

____

4 テレビ演説をする２組とはどういう４人ですか？

____

5 Winner-take all system を説明しなさい。

____

6 就任式で大統領が行うことを挙げなさい。

____

Notes

1 exert influence on ... …に影響を及ぼす　outsized かなり大きな　Members of Parliament 国会議員
2 eligible 有資格の　consecutive 連続した（形容詞）
3 candidate 候補者　a primary election 予備選挙　caucus（政党支部の）幹部会議　a nominating convention 指名会議
4 nominee 指名を受けた人・候補者
5 poll 投票所　elector 選挙人
6 Inauguration Day 大統領就任日　oath 誓約　outline 概説する　administration 施政

2 Fill in the blanks to summarize each paragraph.

A presidential candidate must be a person who is a natural-born citizen of the U.S., at least 1(t) years old, and a permanent resident in the U.S. for at least fourteen consecutive years. A president cannot be elected for more than two 2(f) terms. The first step in the process is 3(l) elections, in which each party chooses a candidate for the presidency through vote or discussion. Then, at the national level, each party holds a 4(n) conventions to choose its candidate. Step 3 is the stage where candidates appear on TV and give speeches and take part in 5(d) to appeal to voters. The election for the 6(p) vote is held early in November. The new president takes the 7(o) of office on January 20 of the following year.

3 Which party does the following statement explain, the Democratic Party or the Republican Party? (The difference is not mentioned in the paragraph)

A. This party supports free markets and limited government, opposing regulation and labor unions, and supporting conservative policies.

→ the ( ) Party

B. This party supports a mixed economy by providing government intervention and regulation in the economy.

→ the ( ) Party

Cause and Effect

原因から結果へ

10

エッセイの構成：フロー型

❶ トピックの紹介

フロー

❷ 原因 → ❸ 結果

❹ まとめ・コメント

ボディとなるパラグラフが、原因→その結果、と進むエッセイパターン。何かの事象があり、それが原因となってあることが起こる、その過程を説明するものです。8課の「歴史をたどる」と9課の「過程を説明する」は流れの過程に重きをおいたものですが、本課は起点と終点のみにフォーカスをあてたものです。同じ時系列のくくりに入れられていますが、本文を読んでみると全く違うテイストになっていることに気づくはずです。

A. Uganda : a Banana Republic

20

1 Have you ever wondered what people in the African nation of Uganda live on? Well, to put it in a nutshell, they live on bananas. In the same way as Japanese people eat rice every day, Ugandans eat bananas every day. Now, if your staple food, whether it's rice or bananas, is threatened, it becomes a serious problem. If your staple food were to disappear, would you be able to give it up and change to an alternative food? Or, if you knew that your staple food might harm your health, would you dare to continue to eat it?

2 In Uganda, a typical adult eats at least three times his or her weight in bananas each year! They eat bananas raw, of course, but they also often steam, boil, and roast them. They even turn bananas into gin and beer. Uganda's production of bananas is second only to that of India, but considering the size of Uganda's population, and how many bananas it consumes, Uganda can truly be called "the banana republic!" Bananas account for more than 30 percent of Ugandans' daily calorie intake. With a single plant lasting many years and providing a large bunch of fruit every few months, bananas are a key crop in Uganda. The main banana species is matoke, a long green banana that is usually steamed and mashed and then eaten with beans, peanut sauce, or meat.

3 But now, Uganda's bananas are under threat. In recent years, a devastating bacterial disease known as banana xanthomanas wilt, or BXW, has swept across Uganda and its neighboring countries. The rapid spread of BXW, which destroys the entire plant and contaminates the soil around it, has endangered the livelihoods of millions of farmers who rely on bananas. BXW is transmitted by insects and wasps, and the traditional use of banana leaves to cover the bunches of fruit heading to market has accelerated the spread of this dreadful bacteria.

4 To protect their staple food, Ugandans must decide whether to begin growing genetically modified (GM) bananas, which, thanks to science, is now an option. GM researchers have been able to add a sweet pepper gene to various vegetable plants, improving their resistance to disease. The gene produces a protein that kills cells infected by disease-spreading bacteria. Laboratory tests on genetically modified bananas incorporating this technique have been highly promising, with six out of eight strains proving 100 percent resistant to BXW. GM crops are still banned in Uganda, however, and the scientists had to get special permission just to conduct their tests. Academia Sinica, the Taiwanese research institute that pioneered the sweet-pepper-gene technology, agreed to issue a royalty-free license. Other GM banana experiments are under way in Uganda, including one that aims to fortify the fruit with iron and vitamin A.

5 It would be easy to introduce GM bananas to save the Ugandan people from hunger and the country from economic disaster. But some people are worried that in

the long run, this may have disastrous consequences. Many people are still against GM food, but do the Ugandans really have any other choice?

❶ 前の文章をまとめてみよう。

① 導入 1
主食が危機に陥ったらどうしますか？

→

② 導入 2
ウガンダ人の主食＝(　　　　　　　　　　)

↓

③ 原因

←

④ 結果

↓

⑤ まとめ

❷ Fill in the blanks to summarize each paragraph.

1 Ugandans live on bananas, but now bananas are (t　　　　　　　　　　).

2 Bananas represent 30 percent of Ugandans' daily (c　　　　　　　　　　) intake.

3 Bananas in Uganda are now under threat because of a devastating (b　　　　　　　　　　) disease.

4 GM foods are prohibited in Uganda, but now, to (p　　　　　　　　　　) their bananas, Ugandans are thinking of introducing GM bananas.

5 Many Ugandans are worried that in the long run, introducing genetically modified bananas may have disastrous (c　　　　　　　　　　).

Notes

1 live on ... …を主食とする　to put it in a nutshell 要するに　staple food 主食　alternative 代替の
2 account for ... …を占める　intake 摂取　a bunch of 一房の　mash つぶす
3 xanthomanas wilt かいよう病　contaminate 汚染する　endanger 危機にさらす　livelihood 生計　wasp スズメバチ
4 sweet pepper ピーマン　incorporate 取り入れる　strain 種(しゅ)　royalty-free 特許権の生じない(形容詞)　fortify 強化する

B. Detroit Bankruptcy

21

1 In July 2013, Detroit announced that it was filing for bankruptcy, which shocked not only the United States but also the entire world. Detroit is the most populous city in the state of Michigan, and has long represented America's "national pride"—the automobile industry. Detroit was once known as the "Paris of the Midwest" and had the nation's highest per capita income. Yet this very same prosperous city has now gone "belly up." How could this have happened?

2 The city was settled in 1701, making it one of the oldest cities in the U.S. Midwest. During the 19th century, Detroit grew into a thriving hub for commerce and industry, taking advantage of transportation resources such as the Detroit River and a parallel rail line, as well as the Great Lakes. Around the start of the 20th century, entrepreneurs in the Detroit area—notably Henry Ford—began the manufacture of automobiles. Later, Detroit's auto industry was an important element of the American "Arsenal of Democracy" that supported the Allied powers during World War II.

3 But after reaching a peak in the 1950s, Detroit gradually declined. According to 2010 U.S. Census data, Michigan lost 48 percent of its manufacturing jobs during the 2000-2010 decade. What are the reasons for this precipitous decline? First, the U.S.'s dominant position as the world's leading auto maker, with Detroit at its center, was threatened by foreign automobile manufacturers, especially Toyota of Japan. Second, many researchers point out that because of the North American Free Trade Agreement with Canada and Mexico (known as NAFTA), millions of U.S. manufacturing jobs were lost, with Detroit hit particularly hard. A third factor in Detroit's fall has to do with the growing number of U.S. immigrants. The overall development of the U.S. economy and then the automobile industry led to rising demands for labor in Detroit, which were filled by huge numbers of newcomers. A variety of nationalities made for a complex situation in the city, which led to an increase in unrest and crime. Rich whites started to move out of Detroit, leaving the poorer classes behind, and accelerating the city's economic decline. Today, Detroit has the worst of all possible employment scenarios: a poorly qualified workforce and very few job opportunities available.

4 Detroit has been devastated by the economic decline. The murder rate is at a 40-year high, only a third of its ambulances are in working order, and nearly half of its streetlights are broken. Citizens wait 58 minutes for the police to respond to calls, compared with a national average of 11 minutes. There are 78,000 abandoned buildings in a city of 360 square kilometers. Detroit's "inner city" areas are mostly populated by the poor, ethnic minorities who rely on economic support from the government. Many rich white people have left Detroit in search of better jobs, and many others live in the city's suburbs, isolating themselves from the poor immigrants living in Central Detroit.

5 The city's attempts to recover had little or no real effect, and Detroit ended up filing for Chapter 9 bankruptcy on July 18, 2013, the largest municipal bankruptcy filing in U.S. history, with debts estimated at between 18 and 20 billion dollars. No other major U.S. city has ever filed for a Chapter 9 bankruptcy. New York, Cleveland, and Philadelphia all came close, but all brokered last-minute deals rather than face the hard cuts and legal fight that a Chapter 9 filing triggers. Detroit's situation was so dire, however, that it had no choice but to go bust and reorganize its debts in the bankruptcy court. Current statistics tell the whole story. Sixty percent of all of Detroit's children are living in poverty. Fifty percent of the population is functionally illiterate. A third of Detroit's 140 square miles is vacant or derelict. Eighteen percent of the population is unemployed. Only 10.6 percent of Detroit's residents, according to the 2010 U.S. Census, considered themselves white.

6 The action of a major city's filing for bankruptcy is desperate sounding and unconventional, but many large companies that have announced bankruptcy (including giants like GM and Chrysler) have made successful recoveries. Will it work for Detroit, too?

Notes

1 file for bankruptcy 破産を申し立てる　populous 人口の多い　per capita income 一人あたりの収入　prosperous 繁栄した（形容詞）　go belly up 破産する

2 thriving 繁栄した（形容詞）　hub 中心　entrepreneur 企業家　notably とりわけ　Arsenal of Democracy「民主主義の兵器庫」　the Allied powers 連合軍

3 precipitous 急な　unrest 不穏　a poorly qualified workforce 未熟練労働者　available 手に入る（形容詞）

4 devastate 荒廃させる　be in working order 正常に働いている　in search of ... …を探して　isolate oneself from ... …から距離をおく

5 end up ~ing ～に終わる　municipal 市の　broker a deal 取引をまとめる　trigger 引き起こす　dire 悲惨な　go bust 破産する　illiterate 文盲の　derelict 見捨てられた

6 desperate sounding 絶望的に聞こえる　unconventional 異例の

❶ それぞれの段落について、次の質問に答えなさい。

1 2013年にデトロイトが世界を驚かせた事件とは？

____

2 デトロイトを有名にした最も有名な企業は何ですか？

____

3 デトロイトを衰退に導いた理由を３つ簡潔に書きなさい。

① ______________________________

② ______________________________

③ ______________________________

4 経済的衰退のせいでデトロイトはどういう状態になっていますか？ いくつか具体例を書きなさい。

____

____

5 経済的衰退のせいでデトロイトがとった最後の手段とは？

____

6 これからの見通しに関して筆者はどう言っていますか？

____

❷ Choose the two factors mentioned in the passage that have led to Detroit's decline.

(　　) (　　)

a. The success of Japanese Toyota.
b. The North American Free Trade Agreement (NAFTA) was agreed to between the U.S., Canada, and Mexico.
c. Detroit's automobile manufacturers supported the Allied powers during World War II.
d. Rich white people left Detroit.

❸ Fill in the blanks with numbers.

1. Detroit was settled in (　　　　).
2. Detroit reached its economic peak in the (　　　　).
3. During the 2000-2010 decade, (　　　　) percent of manufacturing jobs were lost in Michigan.
4. In the U.S. on average, people have to wait an average of (　　　　) minutes for an ambulance to arrive after they make a call.
5. Detroit's debt is estimated to be between (　　　　) and (　　　　) billion dollars.
6. Some (　　　　) percent of Detroit's population is estimated to be functionally illiterate.

TRY

Write your own Essay!!

つぎのタイトルでエッセイの構成を考えてみよう。

この課で扱ったエッセイ構造を使って、自分でエッセイ構造を考えてみよう。次のエッセイタイトルを使って簡単にエッセイ構造を考え、ポイントを日本語で書いてみよう。余裕があればそれを英文のエッセイにしてみよう。

8 History

1. 国際連合の歴史
   Write a brief history of the United Nations.
2. コンピュータゲームの歴史
   Write a brief history of computer games.
3. 日本のアニメ映画の歴史
   Write a brief history of Japanese animated films.
4. 戦後の日本の歴史
   Write a brief history of post-war Japan.

9 Process

1. 地球温暖化のプロセス
   Explain how global warming came about.
2. 野球のやり方
   Explain how baseball is played.
3. インターネットショッピングのやり方
   Explain the steps involved in shopping online.
4. 「スキヤキ」の作り方
   Explain how to make "sukiyaki."

10 Cause and Effect

1. 日本におけるファストフード店人気の状況と結果
   The popularity of fast-food restaurants and its effect in Japan
2. 学校でのいじめの状況と結果
   School bullying and its effect
3. 日本における少子高齢化の状況と結果
   The declining birth rate and its effect in Japan

Part IV

エッセイ構成：マルチ展開型

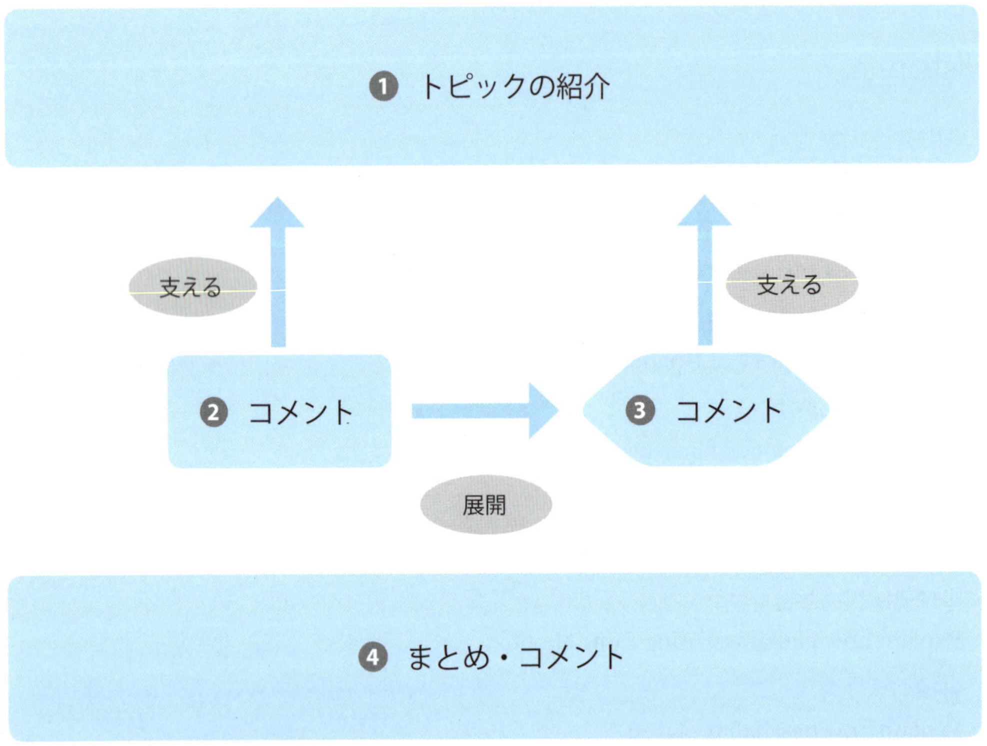

Part IV のエッセイパターンは、それぞれのパラグラフが別個のものとして独立しているのが特徴です。複数の分野からトピックについての説明を行います。このパートでは、「問題の説明―それに対する解答」、「気になる言葉の意味・定義―その背景や社会事情」、「実験―その分析」、「新製品―その背景・エピソード」の4課を扱います。これまでに扱った3つのパートではカバーできないエッセイパターンを「マルチ展開型」としてまとめました。

Problem Solving

問題解決

11

エッセイ構成：マルチ展開型

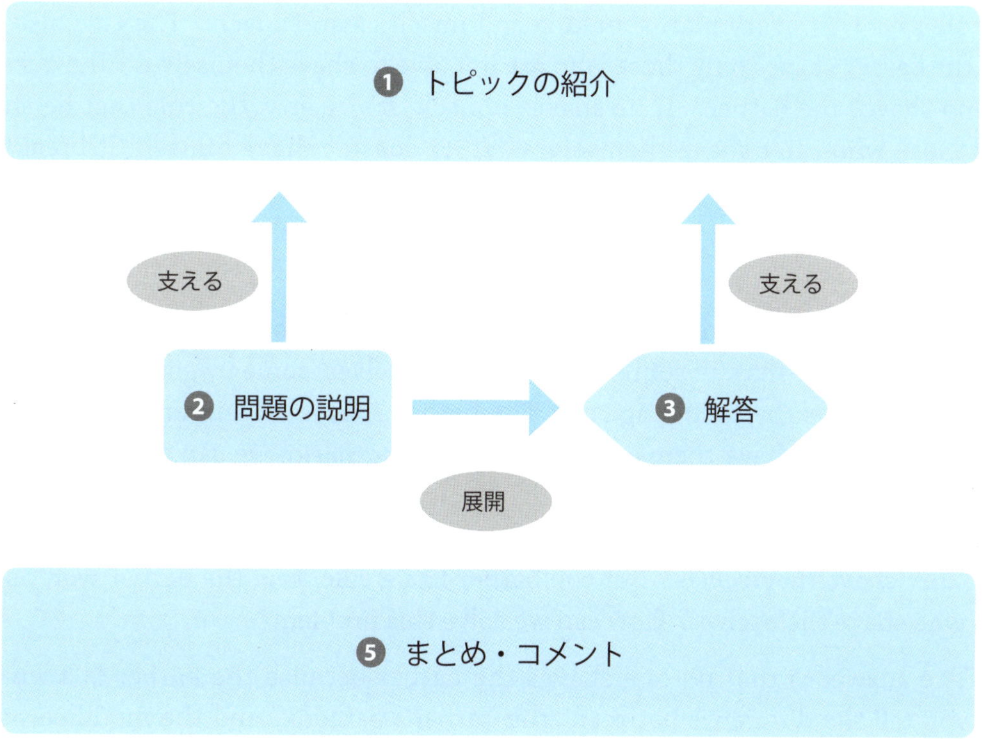

パズルやクイズ、謎を提示し、それを解決するエッセイパターン。まずその問題を詳しく説明して、そのあとで解決方法、解答を説明します。様々ななぞなぞやクイズを目にしたことがあるはず。解答を聞いて、「やられた」と感じたことなどありませんか？ここでは「床屋のパラドックス」と「モンティ・ホール問題」を紹介しています。皆さんはこれらの問題解けますか？「問題の提示」と「それに対する解答」が別個のパラグラフとして、それでも密接な関係をもって展開していきます。

A. "Paradox"

22

1 The word "paradox" is used to describe an apparent contradiction that actually expresses a single truth. An example would be two things that both appear to be true but that when they are set alongside each other appear to be in contradiction.

2 Here, I would like to introduce one well-known paradox called "the barber's paradox," which is also sometimes called Russell's Paradox because the British philosopher/mathematician Bertrand Russell highlighted a similar theory. The paradox goes like this. There is only one barber in a certain town. In this town, an old rule says that every man should keep himself clean-shaven. The rule also says that the barber shaves only those who are not able to shave themselves. The question is, who shaves the barber? If he shaves himself, it's against the rule that he shaves only those who can't shave themselves. If he doesn't shave himself, it breaks the town's rule that every man should keep himself clean-shaven. This is a paradox. This paradox can, however, be modified into the following puzzle, which will render it no longer a paradox.

3 Suppose there is a town with just one barber. In this town, every man should keep himself clean-shaven: some by shaving themselves, some by going to the barber. The barber obeys the following rule: The barber shaves all and only those men in town who cannot shave themselves. Under this scenario, we can ask the following question: who shaves the barber? If there is no other barber in the town, the barber can't be shaved, since it is against the town's rule that the barber shaves only those who can't shave themselves. But the barber has a rule, too: the barber won't shave men who shave themselves. How can we solve this problem?

4 The answer is that no one shaves the barber because the barber is a woman. Can you tell the difference between "the barber's paradox" and the modified puzzle above? In the paragraph of "the barber's paradox," "the barber" is replaced by "he" or "himself." This means the barber is clearly a man. However, in the modified puzzle, there is nothing to suggest that the barber is or has to be a man. People tend to assume that barbers are always men. But this is not true. This is an example of how prejudice or fixed ideas can often prevent us from thinking clearly.

5 We have seen that a paradox is a situation where two apparently true statements are incompatible. But a quiz or puzzle, on the other hand, always has a loophole somewhere, and we enjoy finding it. Sometimes it is found in the words that are used; sometimes it is found in the content itself. But the loophole—the way out—is always there waiting for us to find it. That's what makes puzzles so much fun.

❶ 前の文章をまとめてみよう。

①トピック → ②パラドックスの例 ↓

③パズルの例 → ④解答 ↓

⑤まとめ

❷ Fill in the blanks to summarize each paragraph.

1 A "paradox" is a word or statement that explains a situation in which (t   ) things contradict each other.

2 One example of a (p   ) is "the barber's paradox." The first statement is "Everyone should keep himself clean-shaved in a certain town, and the second statement is that there is only one barber in town, and he can shave only those who can't shave themselves."

3 "The barber's paradox" can be made into a puzzle: "Who (s   ) the barber?"

4 The answer is that the barber is a (w   ).

5 The difference between a paradox and a puzzle is that a puzzle has a (l   ) somewhere, the finding of which makes a puzzle so much fun.

Notes

1 apparent 見せかけの　contradiction 矛盾　alongside ～と並んで(前置詞)
2 highlight とりあげる　clean-shaven ひげをきれいにそって(形容詞)　render A B AをBにする
3 obey 従う　scenario シナリオ
4 replace 置きかえる　prejudice 偏見　fixed idea 固定観念
5 incompatible 矛盾する(形容詞)　loophole 抜け道　content 内容　the way ont 出口

B. Monty Hall Problem

23

[1] The Monty Hall Problem arose from an American television game show called "Let's Make a Deal." The problem's name comes from the name of the show's host, Monty Hall. This show, however, was actually not the first instance of this problem being raised or introduced. Originally, the problem came up in 1975 in a letter written by a man named Steve Selvin to an American statistician. It was published in 1990 as the answer to a reader's question in the "Ask Marilyn" column in *Parade* magazine.

[2] The question goes like this. You are on a TV game show. The host shows you three doors and says that there is a car behind one of the three doors, and that there are goats behind the other two. Your aim is, of course, to win the car as a prize. The host tells you to choose one door. The host does not open your door, but instead he opens one of the other two doors to show you that there is a goat behind it. The host then says that you have a chance to change your mind. You can drop your first chioce and can choose the other door. Will you stay with the door you initially chose? Or will you change your mind and pick the other door? Most of us would probably think that it makes no difference, whether we stay with our first choice or change. Once one door is opened and there is a goat behind it, our chance of winning the car is now 50:50, we think.

[3] But the answer is: "You should change!" If you change to the third door (which you didn't choose at first), you will have a 2-in-3 chance of winning the car. If you stay with the initial door, your chance of winning will be only 1-in-3. Are you convinced? There are several approaches to solving the Monty Hall problem. If you can't understand it, just consider the original unchosen doors as one. And once one of the doors is opened, you have a 2-in-3 chance of winning. The host knows where the car is. He doesn't touch the door you chose, but touches the other two doors and opens one that hides a goat, which raises the possibility of the other hiding the car. If you are still puzzled, consider the same problem with 100 doors instead of just three. You pick a door. The host opens the doors one by one, all those except the door you chose. After he opens 98 doors, he leaves two doors; one that the host didn't open deliberately and the door you chose. Still, do you stay with the door you first chose? Now, the possibility of your winning the car is 1:99. You should definitely change before the last door is opened! I hope you now understand.

[4] When advice-columnist Marilyn answered, "You should change," many people, among them mathematicians and scientists, said this was wrong. I wonder how many readers of this essay agree with this final answer. If the host doesn't know where the car is, the answer would be different. But the point of this problem is that the host *does* know where the car is, and he deliberately removes an obstacle for you.

❶ それぞれの段落について、次の質問に答えなさい。

1 The Monty Hall Problem はもともと誰が誰に出した問題ですか？

2 The Monty Hall Problem では３つのドアのひとつに車が隠されていますが、解答者がひとつ選んだ後、司会者は何をしますか？

3 解答者は、自分が最初に選んだ答えに固執するべきですか、それとも変えるべきですか？

4 このパズルの重要なところはどこですか？

Notes

1 make a deal 取引をする　statistician 統計学者　column コラム
3 deliberately 意図的に
4 remove 取り払う　obstacle 障害

❷ True or False questions.

1. In the TV game show, if you choose a door with a car behind it, the host will immediately open that door. T F

2. There are three doors in the TV game show; one with a goat behind it, another with nothing, and the other with a car. T F

3. It makes no difference whether you stay with the door you chose at first or change to the other door. T F

4. According to the passage, the possibility of winning a car is 50:50 after the host opens the first door that has a goat behind it. T F

5. After the host opens the door with a goat, you are allowed to change to the door that you didn't choose at first. T F

❸ Fill in the blanks.

If you want to win the car, you should drop the door you first chose and change to the other door. After the host opens the second door with a goat behind it, you have a greater possibility of winning a car with the 1(o   ) door than with the first door you chose. You will have a 2(b   ) chance, not a 50-50 chance, if you change. If you stay, your chance will be only 3(   ). The important point of this game is that the 4(h   ) knows where the car is. By opening the first door, the host gives you a 2-in-3 chance for the third door. Therefore, you should choose the third door!

Definition of a New Word

最近気になる言葉を考えよう

12

エッセイ構成：マルチ展開型

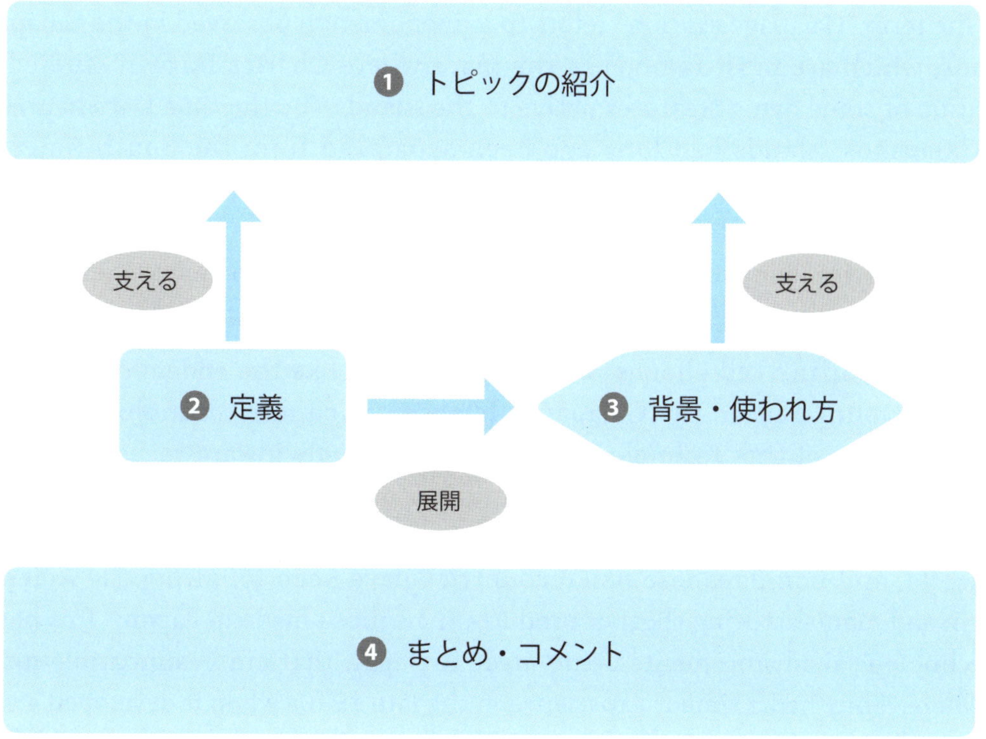

テレビ・雑誌・新聞などで最近よく聞く・見る言葉はありませんか？もともとはどういう意味なのか知ってますか？その元来の意味を基にして、現在はどのように使っているのかを考えてみましょう。また、なぜその言葉がはやっているのかを考えてみましょう。「気になる言葉のもともとの意味、現在の用法」と「その言葉がどういう社会事情で使われるようになったか」が、別々のパラグラフでありながら密接な関係をもって展開していきます。

A. "Galapagos Syndrome"

24

1 According to some economic analysts, Japan has been suffering from what has been termed a "Galapagos syndrome." This phrase applies in particular to the current phenomenon of Japanese cell-phone manufacturing. Japan once enjoyed greater economic prosperity than it does now, and it is still true that Japan's technology is rated first in the world. But this can sometimes lead a country in the wrong direction. The Japanese cell-phone and smart-phone industry is a good example of this. What exactly is meant by the "Galapagos syndrome" or "Galapagosization?"

2 The term "Galapagosization" refers to a phenomenon observed in the Galapagos Islands, which are most famous as the place where Charles Darwin studied the evolution of some living creatures native to the islands. By the time Darwin arrived, the Galapagos Islands had long ago been separated from the South American continent. They had also been isolated from the rest of the world—until Western explorers eventually found them. By the 1800s, as Darwin found, the many animal and plant species living on those islands had evolved in their own way—endemically and in complete genetic isolation from those species found in other locations.

3 Back to Japan's cell-phones, which are in a way like the endemic species that Darwin encountered on the Galapagos Islands. Japanese technology outpaced global adoption of that technology, and the increasingly inward focus of Japanese cell-phone manufacturers led to the creation of industry standards that were incompatible with universal standards. U.S. cell-phone software has dominated the world, and non-Japanese Asian countries have been following the American system and manufacturing cheaper products than those made in Japan. This has led to technological advancements being made in Japan that are incompatible for use elsewhere. Sony had a similar experience in the late 1970s when it developed a video system called "Betamax." Sony was confident that video player makers would follow its lead, but they didn't: they chose the VHS system over Sony's Betamax. In the game industry, Sony's PlayStation was counterattacked by Microsoft's Xbox. Sony, as everybody can agree, has top-class technology, but some critics are now saying that the company should "tone their technology down" and make their products easier for outside developers to use. Unfortunately, recent developments in the world economy have been speeding up this "Japan-only" trend. The rising value of the yen has raised the prices of Japanese products and made it difficult to export them.

4 Today, the term "Galapagosization" refers to something excellent but whose very excellence makes it difficult to use outside a certain area or group. Traveling abroad has long been very popular with Japanese young people, but nowadays many are content to stay within Japan, where they can buy and use their own products—their own Japanese-made video games, DVDs, computers, and anime. Some people are concerned that this isolating trend among young Japanese might be another example of "Galapagosization."

❶ 左の文章の内容をまとめてみよう。

① 導入：とりあげる言葉

→ ②「ガラパゴス化」の定義

↓ ③ 現在どのように使用されているか？

← ④ まとめ

❷ Fill in the blanks to summarize each paragraph.

1 The word "(G　　　　　　　　　)" is introduced using Japanese cell-phones as an example.

2 The original meaning of the word comes from the Galapagos Islands, where many isolated plant and animal (s　　　　　　　　　) evolved in their own unique ways.

3 Like many species in the Galapagos Islands, Japan's (c　　　　　　　　　)-phones have evolved in their own unique ways, making them very different from other cell-phone models manufactured around the world.

4 The word "Galapagosization" is now used to refer to something that is incompatible with use (o　　　　　　　　　) a certain area or group.

Notes

1 analyst アナリスト（分析家） term ～と呼ぶ syndrome 症候群 apply to ... …にあてはまる manufacturing 製造業 prosperity 繁栄 rate 評価する

2 refer to ... …を意味する evolution 進化 native to ... …固有の species 種 endemically 特有な状態で genetic 遺伝的な

3 endemic 特有の outpace ～より先に行く adoption 採用 inward 国内志向の incompatible 折り合わない(形容詞) counterattack 反撃する critic 批評家 tone ~ down ～を下げる

4 be content to V ～することに満足している

B. Rare Earth

25

[1] The term "rare earth" suddenly grabbed Japanese people's attention in September 2010 when China announced that it was reducing its exports of rare metals, an action that came in response to a shipping incident in the Japan Sea. At the time, except for a few experts or computer industry employees, most of us had no idea what "rare earth" was or meant. So let's take a quick look at what "rare earth" metals are and why they are so important.

[2] Rare earth minerals (or rare earth elements) are a set of seventeen special chemical elements—specifically, the fifteen lanthanides plus scandium and yttrium. Despite being fairly abundant, rare earth minerals are quite difficult to mine and extract, which makes them relatively expensive. Their industrial use was limited until the late 1950s and early 1960s. The reason why so many countries covet these rare earths is that they are used in mobile phones and computers, with their use expanding rapidly into many other fields. To put it succinctly, they are becoming indispensable in all the most "cutting edge" technologies.

[3] Until 1948, most of the world's rare earths were derived from placer sand deposits in India and Brazil. Throughout the 1950s, South Africa was the world's most common source of rare earth minerals. During the 1960s and up until the 1980s, the Mountain Pass rare earth mine in California was the leading producer. Today, China accounts for over 97 percent of the world's rare earth supply. Most of this comes from Inner Mongolia.

[4] New demand for these elements has recently strained supplies, and there is growing concern that the world may soon face a shortage of rare earths, concerns that have intensified with certain recent actions on the part of China. Specifically, China has implemented curbs on exports and a crackdown on smuggling. On September 1, 2009, China announced plans to reduce its export quota to 35,000 tons per year between 2010 and 2015, ostensibly to conserve scarce resources and protect the environment. China, it seems, has now realized the great value of rare earths and has begun to use them as a political tool, just as it did with oil in the past.

[5] In response to China's announcement, scientists and politicians worldwide are seeking other ways to get their hands on rare earth elements. So far, there seem to be three possible sources. One is to seek other places to mine. Australia, Brazil, Canada, South Africa, Greenland, and the United States are all candidates. And in 2011, Yasuhiro Kato, a geologist at the University of Tokyo who led a study of Pacific Ocean seabed mud, published results indicating that the mud could hold rich concentrations of rare earth minerals. The second way is recycling. New advances in recycling technology have made the extraction of rare earths from other used materials more feasible, and several recycling plants are currently operating in Japan. These plants are expected to be able to eventually produce 200 tons a year of rare earths from

used fluorescent lamps, magnets, and batteries. The third way is to employ nuclear reprocessing. Nuclear fission of uranium or plutonium produces a full range of elements, including all their isotopes. But the radioactivity of many of these isotopes makes it problematic that extracting them can be done safely and economically. So the question remains: Will Japan be able to find an efficient way to secure a supply of rare earths?

1 それぞれの段落について、次の質問に答えなさい。

1 「レアアース」という言葉が急にとりあげられるようになったのは何がきっかけですか？

____

2 レアアースとは何か、説明しなさい。

____

3 レアアースを産出してきた国を年代順に書きなさい。

____

4 中国がレアアース輸出を減らした本当の意図は？

____

5 レアアースを得る３つの可能性とは？

① ____________________

② ____________________

③ ____________________

Notes

1 grab 掴む　in response to ... …に呼応して　incident 事件

2 specifically 具体的に言うと　lanthanide ランタノイド　scandium スカンジウム　yttrium イットリウム　abundant 豊富な　mine 採掘する　extract 抽出する　covet ほしがる　to put it succinctly 簡潔に言うと　indispensable 不可欠な　cutting edge 最新の

3 be derived from ... …からくる　placer sand 砂鉱　deposit 鉱床

4 strain 引き締める　intensify 強くなる　on the part of ... …の側からの　implement 実行する　curb on ... …の制限　crackdown 取り締まり　smuggling 密輸　quota 割当　ostensibly 表向きは

5 geologist 地質学者　extraction 抽出　feasible 実行可能な　fluorescent lamp 蛍光灯　employ 採用する　fission 分裂　uranium ウラン　plutonium プルトニウム　isotope アイソトープ　radioactivity 放射能　problematic 問題となるような　secure 確保する

❷ True or False Questions.

1. China has been producing and supplying rare earth metals since 1948. T F
2. South Africa is still the world's leading supplier of rare earth elements. T F
3. In 2009, China started to export rare earths to industrial countries. T F
4. A Japanese geologist found that the mud on the floor of the Pacific Ocean may hold a rich source of rare earth minerals. T F
5. Recycling plants of rare earths are actually working in Japan. T F

❸ Fill in the blanks.

Rare earth minerals are a set of 1(s   ) chemical elements, and the reason why these minerals are called "rare" is that it is quite difficult to 2(m   ) them. Rare earths are wanted by many countries because they are used in the manufacture of mobile phones and 3(c   ). Today, 4(C   ) is the country that produces more rare earths than any other country in the world, and it has now realized the great value of these elements and has started to use them as a 5(p   ) tool to negotiate with other countries.

Experiment
実験で証明

13

エッセイ構成：マルチ展開型

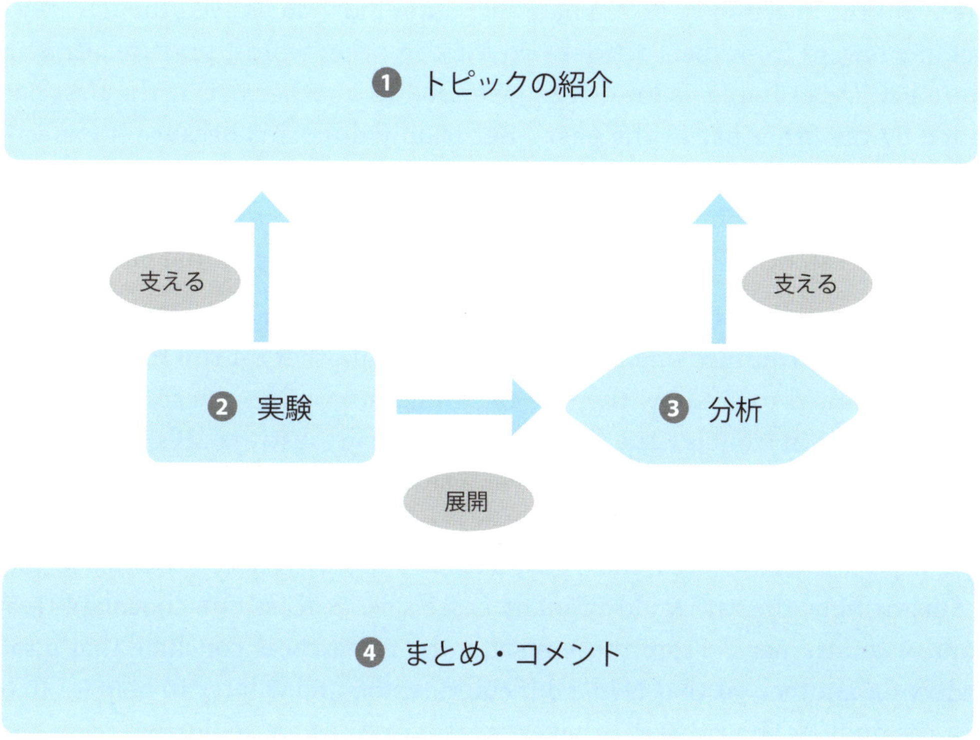

実験によって新しいことが発見される。何かを検証したい、証明したいと思う場合、何かしらの実験や調査を行います。その実験のやり方を詳細に説明し、そのあとでその実験や調査結果から何が言えるのかを分析するエッセイパターンです。「実験の詳細、なぜそれが知りたいのか」、「その実験結果から何がわかるのか」が別々のパラグラフでありながら密接な関係で進んでいきます。

A. Rats also Have Sympathy.

26

1 There are many stories in which animals are compared to humans, stories in which they show similar feelings of anger, worry, sorrow, and so on. If you are a pet owner, you would probably agree that animals are indeed emotional beings. But how far would you go with this assessment? Would you say that animals show sympathy for other individuals and try to help them? You might say that it's natural for animals to protect their own children, sometimes at the cost of their own lives. This is true, because it is animals' instinct to protect their offspring, to allow their species to survive. But the question is, do animals help other individuals even though they can't expect any reward from their action? Do they, in other words, practice altruism? A vampire bat, for example, is known to give food to another bat, if the first bat has been fed by the other bat in the past. But it only does this because it expects the other bat to give it food in return if it, the first bat, becomes hungry in the future. But does this indicate true sympathy on the part of the bat? Or is it just motivated by the expectation of reward? This is what some scientists are trying to find out.

2 Recent research by a group at the University of Chicago conducted the following experiment. They confined one rat in a cage and let another rat run freely outside the cage. They wanted to see how the free rat would respond to the confined rat when the caged rat was in trouble. The free rat, hearing many distress calls from within the cage, tried to open the cage over and over again. The free rat did this even though it could not expect anything in return even if the rat in the cage were released. In a further experiment, the researchers gave a small supply of chocolate chips to the free rat. Surprisingly, the rat would in many cases save at least one chocolate treat for its captive counterpart. From these results, the researchers conclude that a rat can feel sorry for another rat that is in a difficult position and will try to help it. In other words, the findings show that rats have empathy and can act selflessly.

3 The idea that animals have emotional lives and are capable of detecting emotions in others has been gaining ground for decades. Empathetic or even altruistic behavior has been observed in apes and monkeys, and testified to by pet owners (especially dog owners). Recently, scientists have demonstrated "emotional contagion" in mice, a situation in which one animal's stress causes stress in another. But empathy that leads to a helping activity—what psychologists call "pro-social behavior"—had not been definitively shown in non-primates until the Chicago experiment.

4 If animals have feelings of sympathy, a deeper, more abstract question naturally arises: What differentiates human beings from animals? Is it true that there is always a reason behind any animal—including human—action? Why do we feel pity or compassion when we see distressed people? The answer, as has often been explained, is that we feel these emotions because we can imagine another's pain or sorrow, and this affects our own feelings and behavior. If that's the case, then, does helping someone

who is distressed mean that we are actually just trying to reduce our own distress—the distress which comes from seeing someone suffer? And, by extension, does the fact that animals have or show sympathy mean that they can imagine another individual's stress? These questions are some of the most fascinating in biology and behavioral science at the moment, and researchers are hard at work trying to answer them.

❶ 冒頭の文章を使って前のエッセイ構造を確認してみよう。

① 導入：取り扱う疑問は？

____

____

____

→

② 実験

____

____

____

↓

③ 分析

____

____

____

____

←

④ まとめ：もし動物が同情心をもつのなら、どんな問題が出てくるか？

____

____

____

❷ Fill in the blanks to summarize each paragraph.

1 Do animals show (s   ) for other individuals and not just for their own children?

2 An experiment has shown that a free rat tried to rescue another rat that had been locked up in a (c   ) and that it even tried to give its distressed counterpart food.

3 Such helping activity can be seen in (a   ) and monkeys, but in other animals it has not been definitively shown until a recent experiment.

4 If animals are found to have feelings of sympathy, does that mean they can actually (i   ) another individual's stress?

Notes

1 be compared to ... …に例えられる anger 怒り sorrow 悲しみ emotional 感情的な assessment 評価 sympathy 同情 at the cost of ... …を犠牲にして instinct 本能 offspring 子供 species 種 reward 報酬 altruism 利他主義 a vampire bat 吸血コウモリ in return お返しに indicate 示す on the part of ... …による be motivated by ... …に動機づけられる

2 confine 閉じ込める distress 苦悩 release 解放する treat ごちそう captive 捕われた(形容詞) counterpart 相手 empathy 共感 selflessly 自分の利益をかえりみず

3 detect 発見する gain ground 受け入れられる empathetic 共感的な altruistic 利他的な testify to ... …を証言する demonstrate 示す contagion 伝染 pro-social behavior 向社会的行動 non-primate 非霊長類

4 abstract 抽象的な differentiate A from B AをBから区別する compassion 共感 distressed 苦悩する(形容詞) affect 影響を与える reduce 減じる by extension さらに踏み込んで behavioral science 行動科学 at work 仕事をして

B. Indian DNA

1 Since discovering the existence of DNA, scientists have been diligently studying its structure and function. DNA analysis has revealed a number of facts that had been unknown for thousands of years. One example has to do with the DNA of people from India. Analysis of Indians' genes can reveal many interesting and useful things about their ancestors, the origin of their caste system, and their physical problems.

2 Indian people have long been noted for their great diversity. A recent study of their genes now shows us that most Indians today can be traced back to just two distinct ancient populations, one from the north, one from the south. The first group are the ancestors of people who came from Europe or the Middle East; the second group are people from southern Asia. The gene samples the researchers collected showed that almost all Indian people have a blend of these two ancestral groups, with the percentage of the blend, of course, being different in different individuals. According to research conducted by Harvard Medical School geneticist David Reich and his colleagues, genetic diversity among Indians is four times greater than that of Europeans. This probably means that while their ancestors were originally two completely different groups, they divided into many groups after the two original groups mixed, and now each group has been living socially isolated from other groups. Inside each small group, the "members" kept their own genetic traits because they didn't marry into other groups.

3 This discovery tells us a variety of things about India's population. The first is that they are especially vulnerable to genetic diseases. People who live in endogamic (that is, marrying within the group) societies have a very difficult time developing stronger genes against disease. By marrying outside their group, however, they can produce offspring who inherit immune system genes from each parent. Because this doesn't happen in endogamic societies, their members have a high susceptibility to genetic disease.

4 The second thing that the results of the Harvard gene study shows is that this phenomenon may have influenced the development of India's caste system. The caste system has existed in India for centuries, and although great efforts have been made to reduce its divisive nature, it remains active and controversial. What the geneticists now say is that endogamy within castes has kept social groups relatively separate for thousands of years and has defined India's population in genetic terms. As Reich put it, "There are populations that have lived in the same town and same village for thousands of years without exchanging genes." The history of India reinforces this fact. Indian indigenous people, the best known of which were Dravidins, were invaded and conquered by many other peoples, particularly Europeans from the north and various Middle Easterners. This invasion began with the Greeks under Alexander the Great, was followed by Islamic people from the Middle East, and so on. Being in a stronger position, these invaders naturally occupied the higher ranks of the caste system.

According to one study, a higher proportion of higher caste members shares genetic traits with the northern ancestral group. Thus, Indian social groups were divided and fixed at a very early time, and the rigid caste system has kept them separate.

5 The third point that the Harvard DNA analysis implies is that because each group has been independent and separate from other groups, India has not been able to develop a distinct identity as one nation. Of course, there was the movement for independence after World War II, but it was led by a group of intellectuals who had been educated in a Western way. The motivation for fighting for independence was to stop Indians' exploitation by Great Britain and other Western countries. It did not grow out of the people's sense of national identity.

6 These three phenomena are just some examples of what DNA analysis of the Indian people can tell us. History has sometimes been distorted, depending on who or which side wrote it. But DNA analysis doesn't distort: it deals in facts. In the years ahead, DNA analysis will become an ever more important item in the social historian's tool kit.

1 それぞれの段落について、次の質問に答えなさい。

1 インド人の遺伝子の分析によってどんなことがわかるか？

____

2 研究者が集めた遺伝子の分析からわかったことは？

____

3 4 5 この発見でわかったことをまとめなさい。

① ______________________________

② ______________________________

③ ______________________________

6 DNA分析は歴史的記述とどう違いますか？

____

Notes

1 diligently 勤勉に reveal 明らかにする caste system カースト制
2 be noted for ... …で有名である diversity 多様性 be traced back to ... …に起源をたどる population 集団 blend 混合 geneticist 遺伝学者 trait 特徴
3 vulnerable to ... …にかかりやすい endogamic 同族婚の inherit 受け継ぐ immune system 免疫 susceptibility to ... …の影響を受けやすいこと
4 divisive 分裂を生じさせるような controversial 議論をよぶような define 定義する As ~ put it ~の言葉を借りれば reinforce 強化する indigenous 土着の Dravidins ドラビダ人 invade 侵入する conquer 征服する rigid 厳格な
5 imply 意味する distinct 明確な exploitation 搾取
6 distort 歪曲させる deal in 扱う a tool kit 道具一式

❷ Fill in the blanks.

1. The best-known original Indian people are called (   ).
2. According to DNA research, Indian people can be traced back to only (   ) ancestral groups.
3. A society in which people only marry people inside their own community is called an (   ) society.
4. Most higher-ranked people in the caste system were from the (   ).

❸ True or False Questions.

1. Indian people are still neatly divided into two groups. T F
2. Indians' genetic diversity is greater than that of Europeans. T F
3. Thanks to India's great diversity, Indian people have developed an excellent immune system. T F
4. Members of many endogamic societies tend to be better protected from genetic diseases. T F
5. The high diversity of the Indian people has made it hard for them to unite or form a true, distinct national identity. T F

New Product

新製品

14

エッセイ構成：マルチ展開型

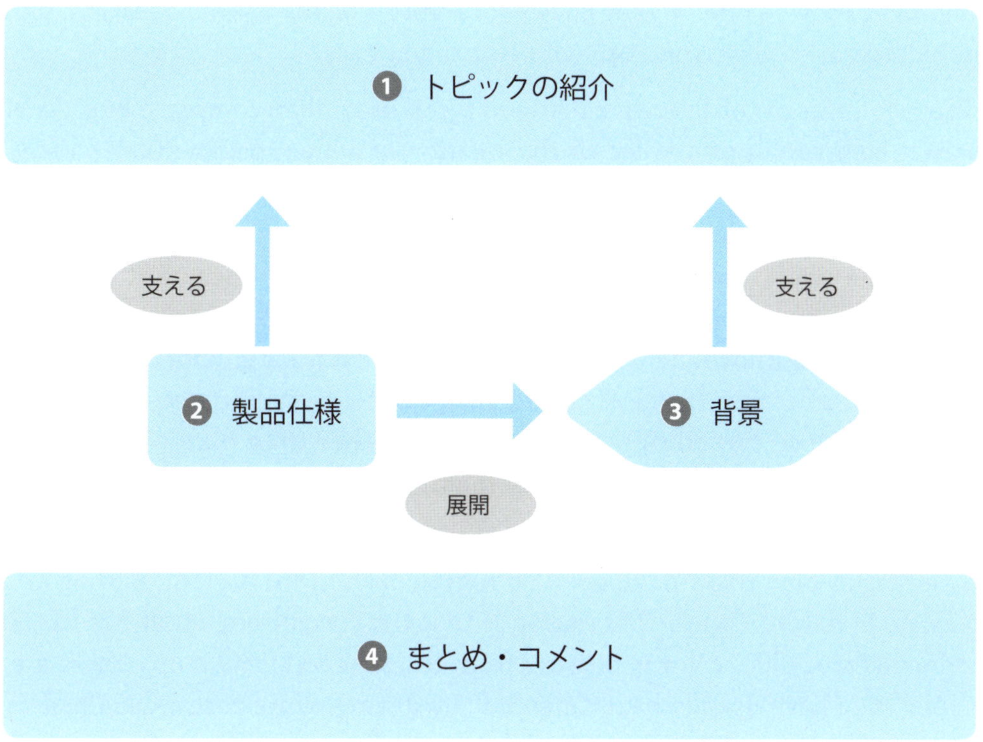

製品の説明はビジネスを行う際には大変重要なものです。新しい製品を説明するためには、まずその製品の詳細や使い方を説明します。そのあとでなぜその製品が必要なのか、どういう使い方をするのか、その製品にまつわる背景、トピックなどを述べます。「製品仕様」、「その製品がでてきた社会的事情やエピソード」という個々のパラグラフでありながら密接な関係をもっています。ここでは「青いバラ」と「コカコーラ」をとりあげています、コカコーラは新製品ではありませんが、それが新製品として登場した経緯とそれにまつわるエピソードを紹介します。

A. Blue Rose

28

1 Even in this day of feminism and gender equality, it is still common for a man to give roses to a woman as a symbol or gesture of his love for her. Lovers have been confessing their love in this way for many centuries. In Europe, on Valentine's Day, it is more customary for men to give their wives, fiancées, or girlfriends roses than it is to give them chocolates. If you were giving someone a special gift of roses, what color would you choose? Red roses (probably the most popular) symbolize passion, white roses stand for purity, and yellow roses represent friendship. But what about blue roses? Might they be one of your choices? Before we look at this question, perhaps we should first ask: "Have you ever even seen a blue rose?"

2 Thirteen years of collaborative research by an Australian company, Florigene, and a Japanese company, Suntory, led to the creation of a blue rose in 2004—a feat that was long thought impossible. Though not exactly blue, it is still being marketed as a blue rose. The companies employed genetic engineering techniques and eventually developed the ability to clone a gene for the "blue" plant pigment delphinidin, which is derived from the petunia. The blue pigment was then inserted into an Old Garden rose—also known as the Cardinal de Richelieu rose. Obtaining the exact hue was difficult because traces of the reddish pigment cyaniding were still present, so initially, the rose turned out to be burgundy rather than blue. Since 1990, the Florigene-Suntory alliance has invested some three billion yen in the development of blue roses, blue carnations, and other blue flowers.

3 The reason blue roses have been so highly desired for so long is that no such thing exists in nature. Why? The reason is that the specific gene that has the ability to produce a "true blue" color is missing from roses' genetic make-up. There are blue roses, but they have usually been "created" by dyeing white roses, usually attained by placing a blue dye into the bark of the roots. In some cultures, blue roses are traditionally associated with royal blood, and thus the blue rose can also denote regal majesty and splendor. In Chinese folklore, the blue rose signifies hope in the face of unattainable love. Because blue roses are "unnatural," they have also come to symbolize mystery and a longing to attain the impossible. Some cultures believe that the wishes of the holder of a blue rose will be granted and that his/her dreams will come true.

4 The two firms are planning to sell one "true" blue rose stem at the exorbitant price of ¥2,000-3,000, about ten times what an ordinary rose goes for. What a high price to pay for true love! How about buying one for your special person? What woman wouldn't love being treated as "special"—or even as royalty—by being presented with such a unique, majestic, and mysterious flower?

❶ 前の文章をまとめてみよう。

① トピック

② 製品の説明

③ 背景

④ まとめ

❷ Fill in the blanks to summarize each paragraph.

1 Roses of all colors have long been important flowers in people's lives, but have you ever seen a (b   ) rose?

2 An (A   ) company and a Japanese company collaborated to create a blue rose by applying (g   ) engineering techniques using blue pigments.

3 Blue roses do not exist in (n   ) because, for genetic reasons, roses don't have blue elements. Thus, blue roses have long been an object of desire.

4 Blue roses are now entering the market, but at an (e   ) price.

Notes

1 feminism 男女同権主義　equality 平等　confess 告白する　customary 一般的な　purity 純粋

2 collaborative research 共同研究　feat 偉業　market 市場に出す　employ 採用する　eventually ついに　clone クローン化する　pigment 色素　delphinidin デルフィニジン　be derived from ... …から引き出される　petunia ペチュニア　insert 入れる　Cardinal de Richelieu リシュリュー枢機卿　hue 色　cyaniding 青化処理　burgundy 暗紅色　alliance 連合　invest 投資する

3 make-up 構成　dye 染める　attain 得る　dye 染料　bark 皮　denote 示す　regal majesty 王者の威厳　splendor 光輝　folklore 民間伝承　signify 示す　unattainable 成就しがたい　longing 憧れ

4 firm 会社　stem 幹　exorbitant 法外な　go for ... …で売れる　royalty 王族　majestic 威厳のある

B. Coca-Cola

29

1 Are you a fan of Coca-Cola? As almost everyone everywhere knows, "Coke" is a product of one of the biggest American companies. When Coke first appeared in America, many people must have been taken aback by its uniqueness, but now Coca-Cola stands as a kind of symbol of American culture, an image promoted mainly through Coke's worldwide ads and commercials.

2 In the late 19th century, a man called John Pemberton invented Coca-Cola as a patent medicine. The patent was bought by a businessman, Asa Griggs Candler, whose marketing tactics led Coke to world dominance of the soft-drink market. Coca-Cola is a strange drink. Most people remember the first time they tried it. It doesn't always make a good first impression. But for some reason, we keep trying it, and some of us can even become addicted to it. Originally, Coca-Cola's two key ingredients were cocaine and caffeine. Cocaine was derived from the coca leaf and caffeine from the kola nut. Hence the name, though it was called Coca-Kola at first, then changed to "Coca-Cola" for marketing purposes. In 1911, the U.S. government took Coca-Cola to court to try to force it to remove caffeine from the drink, but Coca-Cola won. Today, regular "Classic Coke" contains 46 miligrams of caffeine per 12 fluid ounces, while Caffeine-Free-Cola and Diet-Caffeine-Free Cola are just what they say they are—caffeine free.

3 You probably have no idea how Coke is made. Except for a few executives at the center of the company, no one knows the recipe. The ingredients and formula have been kept a closely guarded secret for a long time. This "secret recipe" is actually part of a clever publicity, marketing, and intellectual-property protection strategy. The recipe is supposedly kept in a locked vault. At one point, Coca-Cola used an advertising campaign in which the only two top Coke executives who knew the secret couldn't fly on the same plane—like the U.S. President and Vice-President—in case the plane crashed and the formula was lost forever. A popular myth says that only two Coke executives have access to the formula, with each executive having only half.

4 There have been some attempts by outsiders to discover and then reveal this secret formula. The most recent incident came on February 11, 2011. Ira Glass, a radio host and columnist, revealed on his show that Coke's secret formula had been uncovered in "Everett Beal's Recipe Book," which was reproduced in a 1979 issue of the *Atlanta Journal-Constitution*. The formula is allegedly made from 20 drops of orange oil, 30 drops of lemon oil, 10 drops of nutmeg oil, five drops of coriander oil, 10 drops of neroli oil, 10 drops of cinnamon, and 240 ml of alcohol. Either four or five tablespoons of that flavoring are then mixed with a liter of lime juice, two tablespoons of vanilla, three tablespoons of caramel color, 13.6 kg of sugar, and the fluid extract of coca leaf—plus a small amount of cocaine.

5 Unfortunately, when the recipe is tried, it tastes nothing like today's Coke. Try

it yourself and see what you think. Anyway, Coca-Cola's formula is still one of the world's best-kept and most intriguing secrets.

❶ それぞれの段落について、次の質問に答えなさい。

1 コカコーラはどのような方法でアメリカ文化を代表していますか？

______

2 コーラはなぜ不思議な飲み物だと言っていますか？

______

3 コカコーラの作り方を知っている会社役員はどういう点でアメリカ大統領と副大統領に例えられていますか？

______

4 1979年の「エベレット・ビールのレシピ本」で挙げられているのはなんですか？

______

5 残念なこととは何ですか？

______

Notes

1 be taken aback by ... …に驚く stand as ... …として存在する
2 patent 特許 marketing tactics 市場戦略 dominance 支配的立場 become addicted to ... …中毒となる ingredient 成分 hence 故に take ... to court …を訴える contain 含む fluid ounce 液量オンス
3 formula 処方 publicity 宣伝 intellectual-property protection 知的財産権保護 supposedly おそらく vault 保管室 at one point あるとき myth 神話 have access to 手に入れる
4 allegedly 申し立てによると flavoring 香料 fluid extract 植物抽出液
5 intriguing 興味ある

❷ Fill in the blanks.

Coca-Cola was created by a man called John Pemberton in the 19th century as a patent 1(m　　　　　　　). It was transferred to another owner, who made the drink and his company world famous through his 2(m　　　　　　　) tactics. Since its start, Coke's 3(r　　　　　　　) has been kept secret. A popular myth says that only two executives know it, and they can't 4(f　　　　　　　) on the same plane together. The name Coca-Cola is derived from 5(c　　　　　　　). Some people have tried to reveal Coke's secret formula, but so far none has succeeded.

❸ Answer the following questions in English.

1. What were Coca-Cola's original two key ingredients?

____

2. What was the original spelling of Coca-Cola?

____

3. Why has the Coca-Cola company kept the formula secret?

____

4. Who supposedly revealed Coca-Cola's secret formula in 2011?

____

TRY

Write your own Essay!!

つぎのタイトルでエッセイの構成を考えてみよう。

この課で扱ったエッセイ構造を使って、自分でエッセイ構造を考えてみよう。次のエッセイタイトルを使って簡単にエッセイ構造を考え、ポイントを日本語で書いてみよう。余裕があればそれを英文のエッセイにしてみよう。

11 Problem Solving

1. アルキメデスはどのようにして彼の定理を発見したか？
   Explain how Archimedes discovered the principle of buoyancy.
2. ゴルディアンの結び目をアレキサンダー大王がどのようにして解いたか？
   Explain how Alexander untied the "Gordian Knot."
3. コロンブスはどのようにして卵を立てたか？
   Explain how Columbus made an egg on its tip.

12 Defining New Word

1. ワーキングプアという言葉について説明しなさい。
   What is meant by the phrase "working poor?"
2. 「ニート」という言葉について説明しなさい。
   What is meant by the word "NEET?"

13 Experiment

1. 携帯のない生活をしてみたらどうなるか？
   Explain how your life would be different without a mobile phone.
2. テレビのない生活はどのようなものか？
   What would your life be like if you lived without TV?

14 New Product

1. 近い将来自動販売機にどのような新機能がでてくるだろうか？
   What new vending machine functions will we see in the near future?
2. 携帯にどのような新機能があるとよいですか？
   What new functions would you like to see for your mobile phone?

参照

Lesson 1

"U.S. starts growing fuel-only corn," by Suzanne Goldenberg, GW 8/11/2011
"Right thinking," by Iain Mcgilchrist, GW 22/1/2010

Lesson 2

"At the top of Indian brides' wish-list: a loo," by Emily Wax, GW 30/10/2009
"Alexander the Great rides again to taunt the embattled Greeks," by Helena Smith, GW 19/08/2011

Lesson 3

"Our nightly foreboding," by Richard Wiseman, GW 18/03/2011

Lesson 4

"Light and latitude affect eye and brain size," by Alok Jha, GW 5/8/11
"New form of synchronized swimming," GW 4/3/2011

Lesson 10

"Africa's banana republic turns to GM strains to save staple crop of farmers," by Xan Rice, GW 18/3/2011
"Detroit Bankruptcy," GW 26/7/13

Lesson 13

"Experiment Shows that Rats have feelings too," by David Brown, GW 30/12/11
"The Map of India's Genetic Diversity," GW 23/10/09

Lesson 14

"My love is like a blue, blue rose," by Kathryn Wescott, http://news.bbc.co.uk/2/hi/asia-pacific/8318511.stm
"Radio show 'reveals Coke recipe,'" JT 2/17/2001

*GW: Guardian Weekly
JT: Japan Times

☆ Image credit ☆

p.54　CatLane/istock.com

p.100　NoDerog/istock.com

other all images/isotck.com

Skills for Better Reading <Advanced>		[B-773]
構造で読む英文エッセイ＜上級編＞		
1　刷	2015年 3月 19日	
9　刷	2023年 8月 30日	
著　者	石谷　由美子　　Yumiko Ishitani	
発行者	南雲　一範　Kazunori Nagumo	
発行所	株式会社　南雲堂 〒162-0801　東京都新宿区山吹町361 NAN'UN-DO Co., Ltd. 361 Yamabuki-cho, Shinjuku-ku, Tokyo 162-0801, Japan 振替口座：00160-0-46863 TEL: 03-3268-2311（代表）／FAX: 03-3269-2486	
編　集	加藤　敦	
製　版	木内　早苗	
装　丁	Nスタジオ	
検　印	省　略	
コード	ISBN 978-4-523-17773-9　C0082	

Printed in Japan

E-mail　nanundo@post.email.ne.jp

URL　https://www.nanun-do.co.jp/